Understanding Revelation

A Guide to the End-Times

By Ken Allen

Dedication

To Honor my wife, and Sarah and Rachel, my children.

How to Use this Book

No book written on Revelation should replace the need to read the book of Revelation repeatedly and carefully in a Bible translation of your own choice.

Commentaries and guides can be helpful only when critically reviewed by readers. Men with an imperfect understanding write them. It is recommended that a number of commentaries are read by a variety of authors to gain broad teaching about the subject. God gave teachers within the church because no one person has all the truth of scripture. We are not supposed to exist as Christians in isolation from other Christians. In a multitude of counsellors, there is safety from imbalance and extremism.

The translation of Revelation supplied in this book is a literal translation. Languages do not map word for word across translations. The translator, has therefore, to compromise between strictly rendering the original language and making the translation easily readable. A literal translation is a halfway-house and seeks to show some of the original word order, constructions and meanings but at the expense of a more polished English text. In other words, the English reader looking at the literal translation in this book will, at points, find expressions and word orders that seem strange. It is recommended to compare the literal translation with a readers favourite biblical translation.

There are many references to scriptures within the text of the book. These references are an attempt by the writer to justify statements made. To get the most significant benefit from this book, it is useful for the reader to take the time to look up these references and consider them in their context.

Questions and Feedback

I would be delighted to receive questions and feedback from readers.

It would be most helpful if users identify spelling and grammatical errors to flag this up. Despite rigorous proofreading, these can still exist.

I will try to respond quickly to all issues raised.

I can be contacted at kenallenauthor@gmail.com

My website is www.kenallen.co.uk

My facebook page is www.facebook.com/biblemasterclass

If you have enjoyed reading this book, then please would you consider posting an honest review on Amazon?

Contents

Introduction

Is it Possible to Understand Revelation?

"The way forward is clear."

Problems people have with the book of Revelation

There are many Christians who are not comfortable reading Revelation. There are a number reasons for this. Some find the book to be strange because of its extensive use of imagery, it is dreamlike in its presentation and does not sit comfortably in our Western culture. Because much of the book deals with the future and the end of the world, it can create fear in some readers. A series of apocalyptic films and T.V. programs have linked Revelation to the Horror genre in the minds of many Christians.

There are very many opinions and views as to what the book of Revelation means and some people feel lost in the maze created by so many contradictory teachings. The culture we live in has moved away from believing in absolutes. People with this worldview think that there is no absolute truth. It therefore becomes impossible to come to a definitive conclusion on many issues. True Christians, while believing in the absolute truth of the Bible, can be influenced in a more-subtle way into thinking they cannot come to any conclusions about many of the issues covered by the book of Revelation. There are also some Christians who seem very confident that they know what the book of Revelation means but other people seem equally convinced about views that contradict them. Some immature people can very dogmatically say all sorts of stuff about Revelation which to a number thinking and more cautious Christians can be very off-putting especially when they see Christians, professing to love one-another, becoming hostile and critical of people who disagree with their view of the Second Coming.

Others feel the book is not relevant to their everyday lives. They would reason that unless they are living in the end days of the World it does not concern them. A great emphasis has come into some of our church groupings making the hearers the central focus. The self-help and self-improvement teaching that holds considerable sway in our society has influenced preaching within our churches. While much of this is helpful, it can be tempting to think learning has to be about 'me' for it to be useful and worthwhile.

So, is it possible to understand the book of Revelation? What does the Bible say about this? The short answer to this question is that the Bible teaches we can know in part (1 Corinthians 13:9). In other words, we can understand the book of Revelation but our understanding will be imperfect at this time. Paul says that no man knows anything yet as he ought to know (1 Corinthians 8:2). If we are only willing to learn the things we can entirely understand then we will be very limited in our thinking.

What does it mean to know?

What does it mean to know the book of Revelation? One of the earliest uses of the word 'know' in the Bible refers to Adam having sexual relations with Eve (Genesis 4:1). The word 'know' was used to convey the idea of being intimately joined and of becoming one. Whenever we truly know something, it becomes part of who we are. So, when Jesus said that those who know the truth would be set free (John 8:32), He was referring to much more than a surface head knowledge; He was saying as the disciples become one with the truths of God they will be changed and brought into freedom.

If we wish to understand the book of Revelation this life-changing knowledge is what is needed. Some of the problems that occur with the book are rooted in a head knowledge rather than something that changes people's lives. When I encountered the book of Revelation as a nine-year-old, it radically changed my life and because it so changed my life for good the motivation to discover more about it was increased and led to a better understanding.

Revelation or mind?

Christians have two great mechanisms for knowing the truth. The first is the process of revelation. Revelation is a truth that God reveals to the spirit of an individual. It is not dependent upon the mind but is a work of the Holy Spirit in a person (1 Corinthians 2). It is to the humble and the meek that God gives revelation (1 Peter 5:5). To be humble is the opposite of being proud. The humble want to learn from God. Meek means to be pliable and to be someone who wants to be shaped by God and to follow Jesus. Jesus' disciples were examples of people who were humble and received revelation from God. They recognised that Jesus was the Christ because God chose to reveal this to them (Matthew 16:17). Contrast this with many of the Pharisees and Sadducees. These were proud and, although many of them had a reputation for learning, they could not see that Jesus is the Son of God. The key to understanding the book of Revelation is in the name of the book, revelation.

The second mechanism that Christians have are their minds. We are told to love God with everything we have, including our minds (Matthew 22:37). We will not learn the meaning of Revelation if we do not put our minds to work in searching out what the book means (Psalm 1:2). We do not rely on our minds for revelation, but they are useful servants to us in studying and thinking about the meaning of the book. When God wants to show us truths, it is not an excuse to be passive or careless in our pursuit of what God is saying to us. The mistake that many intelligent people make is to omit the necessity for revelation from God. How many highly talented people have been ungodly and foolish when it comes to the truths of the Bible. The other side of this issue is that we are told to set our minds to work in seeking the teaching of God (Colossians 3:2).

Therefore, we need to read and give time to thinking upon the meaning of the book of Revelation but depend upon God to provide us with the understanding that we need. The value of understanding the book of Revelation is not in our ability to dazzle others with our knowledge but the impact for good it has upon us and our lives.

Hope

Ask a group of people what hope is and they will produce a variety of answers. Some of these might include a feeling of expectation and desire for a particular thing to happen, a sense of trust, or wanting something to happen or be the case. Usually there is an element of uncertainty or even forlornness regarding the issue of hope. My father did the football pools for many years in the hope he would win something, but he never really believed it would happen. In point of fact, he never won more than he paid into the pool. Many people are happy to spend money weekly for the possibility of winning the lottery. Although the chance of winning the jackpot is minuscule people are paying for a small amount of hope as they see it. There are many jokes about the uncertainty of hope. One example conveys the mixed feeling people have about hope with the joke about the optimist falling off the top of the Empire State Building and saying as he passes every window, "Alright so far."

Christian hope is very different to this. The world has devalued the right concept of hope. Biblical hope is an entirely sure thing. It is something that will happen but has not happened yet. Paul makes the point that hope that is seen is not hope (Romans 8:24). The New International Version of the Bible talks about us being sure of what we hope for (Hebrews 11:1). This assurance of future things is at the heart of Christianity but very foreign to our culture. Paul considers hope to be vital and lists it alongside faith and love (1 Corinthians 13:13).

Many Christians have a problem with hope. Many believers struggle with a sense of hopelessness in their lives and churches. Why should this be? During the last fifty years, Christians have increasingly focussed on the here and now. There was a reaction to what was viewed as 'pie in the sky when you die thinking.' Of course, it is essential that we live in the here and now and not over-focus on the future, disengaging from our present lives. As with so many things balance is needed. One of the things that enable us to keep going in current difficult circumstances is the assurance of a better future coming. Paul links patient endurance with hope (Romans 5:4).

Much teaching in our churches is about the hearers living their everyday lives. Other learning is viewed as impractical and not relevant. One of the ways hope is built into people's lives is to teach them the truth about the future. Remember hope is about the future. Christians have the most incredible future ahead of them. It is helpful that we live our current lives in the light of all the beautiful things that lie ahead. The Bible has a lot to say about our future, and the study of this will build hope in our lives. There is nothing for the Christian to fear in what lies ahead. An accurate view of what the Bible teaches about the end times will significantly encourage Christians.

Why Study Revelation?

Revelation occupies a significant part of the Bible. It is the fourth longest book in the New Testament. In chapters, it is longer than Mark and John's Gospels. To not seriously read and study the book of Revelation and its theme of the Second Coming of Christ is to overlook a considerable part of the Bible.

Revelation deals with the end of the world. It is hugely relevant to everybody living in the world. A key feature of this is the fact that each one of us will have to stand before God who will judge us according to the way we have lived. For some, there will be an eternal reward in Heaven. For others, there will be endless punishment in a place described as the Lake of Fire (Amos 4:12).

God has provided the book of Revelation to be profitable for us. Everything in the Bible is to help us. We cannot afford to overlook what God has given us for our help and benefit (2 Timothy 3:16).

God will help us to understand the book. The book of Revelation starts with the words, 'The Revelation of Jesus Christ.' In other words, the book is not a mystery but rather something that God wants to reveal.

There is a promised benefit for those who read and keep the words of the book. Revelation is the only book in the Bible that starts and ends with a promise of blessing for those who read and follow the words of the book (Revelation 1:3, 22:7).

The book of Revelation has a purifying effect on those who believe it. One of the reasons why the Second Coming of Christ is relevant to our everyday lives is because the hope of His coming produces the fruit of purity in our lives (1 John 3:3).

Knowledge of the return of the Lord is a tremendous encouragement to continue and endure in difficulty. An ongoing theme of the book of Revelation is to persevere in hardship. There is a reward to be won from the Lord at His coming. In ignoring the book of Revelation we would ignore much of what God has said to comfort us (James 1:12).

The book of Revelation enables us to avoid deception. One of the features of the return of the Lord will be a deception that many people will suffer. Moreover, this fraud will be deadly. In knowing the book of Revelation, we will be helped to avoid the lies that would swamp us (Matthew 24:4, 5).

It is the Revelation of Jesus Christ. The book of Revelation teaches us about Jesus. To know Jesus is the most important and relevant thing we can do. There are some things said about Jesus that are only in the book of Revelation.

The Holy Spirit will help us understand Revelation. Every true Christian has the Holy Spirit living within them. God has promised us that the Holy Spirit will teach us. The Holy Spirit is well able to show us about the book of Revelation and apply it to our daily lives (1 John 2:27).

The words of this prophecy are not sealed (Revelation 22:10). When Daniel prophesied his words were sealed because the time for their fulfilment was distant. People could not understand these words because the time for understanding hadn't come (Daniel 12:4). However, when Jesus came, the time to understand Daniel's words had also arrived and Jesus unsealed these words (Matthew 24:15). It is evident that God wants us to understand the words of Revelation because they have been left unsealed. There has been a concerted effort by Satan to convince Christians that they cannot understand this book. God here is at pains to underline the fact that the book is open.

Making Sense of Revelation

Read the book but don't try to figure everything out.

Pray to God for revelation and let Him reveal things to you. The more we rely on our wisdom and intellect the more likely we are to invent all sorts of stuff that will not feed us but instead it becomes lifeless knowledge that can make us proud and get us into fights with other Christians.

Don't use the book of Revelation to try and foretell the future.

The heart of this book is the testimony of Jesus rather than a timeline of future events. There is always a danger of abusing Biblical prophecy in an attempt to divine the future. Now prophecy often deals with future matters and God can give insights into this, but He does not give us the whole roadmap to future events or the exact timing of events.

Be tentative.

The Old Testament saints had the great difficulty in trying to figure out what all the prophecies were referring to regarding Jesus' first coming. It was after their fulfilment that Christians were able to see how they all fitted together. It is hardly surprising then that we may have difficulty in understanding how it all works out exactly when dealing with the prophecies of Jesus' return. It is therefore wise to not be too dogmatic about details and situations we have not yet seen.

Understand that a lot of imagery used in the book of Revelation

Revelation is dreamlike in its quality. It is very akin to some of the visions of the Old Testament prophets. Thus, the imagery needs interpreting. The key to interpretation is by seeing how similar images occur in the rest of the Bible. By comparing scriptures with scriptures, we can know the meanings of the pictures. The Bible is consistent in its use of imagery.

It is essential we distinguish between the literal and the figurative.

An example of this is the seven Spirits mentioned before the throne. If we were to take this literally, we would conclude that there are seven Holy Spirits. This conclusion is not the case! The Holy Spirit in other scriptures reveals himself as someone who functions in different ways.

Prophecies can have many partial fulfilments before the complete and perfect events.

There are some excellent Biblical reasons why some prophecy appears to have partial and then a perfect fulfilment. Behind much of the world events, are principalities and powers. In the partial, we often see the echoes of their restrained attempts to fight against us. Another reason for partial fulfilment is a breach (delay) of promise because of unbelief.

Events do not necessarily occur in chronological order.

The images of Revelation are not always in a chronological sequence though often they are.

A picture of what is happening is built up little by little.

We piece together the details of the second coming from a wide range of scriptures. Some writers attempt to give a detailed description of the second coming events to help people do this. These sequences of key features are only useful if people look at the scriptures for themselves and fit the pieces together.

Major Events in Revelation

The Present Age

The church functions on earth by shining light upon Jesus. The Seven churches are denoted as lampstands with Jesus standing in the middle of these forming a circle about Him. The seven churches talk of seven ages through which the church illuminates Jesus to the world (Revelation 1-3).

The Rapture

The Rapture describes the point when Jesus comes to the air and gathers together His church. Living Christians are caught up, and their bodies change into immortal bodies, dead Christians return to life resurrected. This whole company then goes with Jesus to His Father's house, Heaven (Revelation 4:1).

The Tribulation

A seven-year period begins with a wicked world ruler energised by Satan entering into a treaty with the nation of Israel. Things seem to go well but halfway through this period the world ruler breaks the agreement. The world ruler sets himself up as God and demands worship by all with a statue of himself in the rebuilt Jewish temple in Jerusalem. The second half of this seven-year period is called the Great Tribulation which is a time of unprecedented suffering and persecution. If God does not cut this time short, no one will survive the Tribulation. A significant number of people turn to God despite being persecuted and the Good News of Jesus Christ believers proclaim across the earth. This company consists of both Jews and Gentiles (Revelation 4-18).

The Second Coming

The armies of the world gather together for battle in the land of Israel and the Jewish people are facing extermination. At this desperate point the Lord Jesus Christ returns to the Mount of Olives at Jerusalem. He fights against the armies and He destroys them. The Jewish nation will recognise Jesus as their Messiah and find forgiveness and restoration. Jesus begins world rule reigning at Jerusalem. There is a resurrection of the martyred righteous saints who turned to God in the Tribulation. The living nations are also judged at this time when Jesus separates the righteous from the wicked as someone separates sheep from goats (Revelation 19).

The Millennium

Satan is bound for a thousand years in a place called the Abyss; this is a prison for spiritual beings. There follows a period on earth were Jesus reigns and peace and blessing abound. The Kingdom of God has finally come to the world. Despite humanity knowing such a wonderful time many seek to rebel, following Satan's lead, after his release from the Abyss. The rebellion is crushed by God sending fire from heaven upon the people who gather to fight (Revelation 20).

The Final Judgement

Satan finally goes into a terrible place of punishment called the Lake of Fire. The unrighteous are resurrected and stand before a great white throne. There all who have rejected salvation through Jesus are sent forever into the Lake of Fire (Revelation 20).

The Eternal State

The old heavens and earth are burnt up with fire. God creates a new heaven and a new earth. Here people dwell with Jesus forever without any sorrow, death or sin (Revelation 21-22).

The Rapture

What is the Rapture?

The Rapture refers to the church being taken from Earth to be with Jesus. Paul describes this in (1 Thessalonians 4:13-18). The word rapture is from 'rapere' found in the expression "caught up" in the Latin translation of (1 Thessalonians 4:17). Sometimes the rapture is also described by the term 'translation.'

When the church ascends those who are alive are caught up but those who are dead are resurrected and then caught up. God raptured Enoch (Genesis 5:24). Elijah was another Old Testament person raptured (2 Kings 2:11). When Jesus was at the Mount of Olives after His resurrection, he ascended. Jesus was also an example of someone raptured (Acts 1:9). The two witnesses mentioned in Revelation will be resurrected and raptured (Revelation 11:11, 12).

When will the Rapture happen?

There is much disagreement between Christians as to exactly when the Rapture will happen. Some believe Jesus will rapture the church before the seven-year period known as the Tribulation (Pre Tribulationists). Others believe that the church will depart at the end of this period (Post Tribulationists). There are variations of these two views as well. A group of Christians believes that the church will be raptured halfway through the Tribulation (Mid Tribulationists). Another section of the Christians thinks only some of the church will rapture before the Tribulation and the rest at the end of this period (Partial Rapturists).

The implication for those who believe the church leaves before the Tribulation is that Jesus could come at any time (Immediacy). From this point of view, there remains no unfulfilled prophecy to proceed the removal of the church. When I first became a Christian, this is what I believed and still believe, and it was instrumental in my choosing to become a Christian. For people who say that the Church must go through the Tribulation, Jesus cannot come at any time. They believe there are specific prophecies which must be fulfilled before the Rapture since there would need to be at least seven years before this could happen.

Reasons for believing the church will not go through the Tribulation

We do not know when the church will depart. It could happen at any moment. Jesus promised that He would go and prepare a place for His people in Heaven and He promised He would return to take the church to His Father's House. He did not say when this would happen (John 14:2, 3). The idea is of coming for the church and then going to His Father's House. The idea is not going to His church and then down on earth to set up His Kingdom. It is a mistake to link the Rapture of the Church with the Coming of the Lord. Biblically they are not connected, there is a period between the two.

This knowledge that at any moment the Lord could come for His people is a beautiful encouragement (1 Thessalonians 4:18) and (1 John 3:2, 3). Paul in writing to the Thessalonians was encouraging them. It would hardly be encouraging if they had to face the Tribulation before the Rapture.

After the Rapture of the church, there will follow a time on the earth when God begins to judge the sin of the world. This time is a seven-year period known as the Tribulation. The Tribulation will be a time when God's anger is poured out upon the peoples of the earth and will culminate with the Coming of the Lord Jesus Christ. The Tribulation is not to discipline the church but to punish the world. The church will not face the wrath (anger) of God because Jesus died for the sin that we have committed. It is not possible for God to punish our wrongdoing twice (1 Thessalonians 5:9).

The Church is the bride of Christ (Ephesians 5:25). A Hebrew marriage was in three stages. In the first step, the legal marriage took place between the parents of the bride and the groom. The second phase involved the groom removing the bride from the parent's home. Finally, there was a wedding feast. The church already is the bride of Christ, (Romans 7:4). Christ will come for His bride at the Rapture and take her to His Father's house. There will then take place a wedding feast (Revelation 19:7-9).

Jesus speaking to the Philadelphian church promised them deliverance from the world judgment that is coming (Revelation 3:10). The words to specific churches (Revelation 2 and 3) contain teaching for all the assemblies on earth, not just the particular ones in John's time.

The church is absent on earth in Revelation between chapters 4 and 18 which deal with the Tribulation period. The lack of any reference to the church on earth seems unlikely if the church was passing through the Tribulation.

The twenty-four elders (Revelation 4:4) picture the church having been raptured in heaven at a point before the Tribulation begins. We know that it is after the Rapture because they are wearing victors' crowns. Now Paul talks of receiving his victory crown together with everyone else after the Lord appears (2 Timothy 4:8). If the twenty-four elders were saints who had died and gone to be with the Lord before the Rapture, they would not have received their crowns at that point.

If the Rapture happened after the Tribulation, there would be no righteous people left to populate the Millennial Kingdom of Christ. Those living in that kingdom have mortal bodies. Moreover, there would not be a need to separate the sheep from the goats in judgment (Matthew 25:31) because this separation would have already taken place at the time of the Rapture. The Tribulation allows time for a group of people to turn to the truth while still in mortal bodies. These saints will carry on ordinary occupations such as building houses, farming and having children (Isaiah 65:20-23).

The Appointed Seasons

Israel celebrated seven annual feasts. The word feast means appointed season. These appointed seasons picture the appointed seasons of the redemption of the earth (Leviticus 23:4).

The Passover (Leviticus 23:5)

The crucifixion and burial of Jesus is the focus of the Passover. He died on the Passover Day. Biblical days start in the evening and end in the day, for example (Genesis 1:5). The disciples celebrated the Last Supper with Jesus on the night of the Passover (Luke 22:15). The next day was still the Passover, and this was when Jesus died.

Galileans reckoned days as starting in the evening and finishing in the morning. The more Hellenised Jews living in Jerusalem considered days to begin in the morning and end in the evening. It is only in our modern age that the counting of time has become more standardised. The difference in the starting point of the day led to the Northern Jews sacrificing their Passover the day before Southern Jews. The Temple Authorities were happy to accommodate this since it halved the pressure of sacrificing over a quarter of a million lambs in the two-hour time slot they had according to the law. Jesus and His disciples had the Passover Feast in keeping with the other Galileans, but Jesus died as the Southern Jews were sacrificing their Passover lambs in the Temple (MacArthur, 1989, p. 145).

The Feast of Unleavened Bread (Leviticus 23:6-7)

The first and last day of this feast was a Sabbath day and began the next day after the Passover. There were other Sabbath days than the weekly Sabbath. Jesus was three days and nights in the tomb (Matthew 12:40). From this, I would conclude that Jesus died on Thursday, not a Friday. My opinion goes against accepted viewpoints, but it is the only way I can account for the full three days and nights. Also, it solves the problem that many academics have in accounting for one missing day in the chronology of the last week of Jesus' time in Jerusalem before the crucifixion.

Weekday – Days run from evening to morning		
Wednesday Night	Passover Meal, Last Supper	
Thursday Day	Crucifixion and Burial Passover lambs sacrificed	
Thursday Night	High Sabbath, Feast of Unleavened Bread	1st Night
Friday Day		1st Day
Friday Night	Weekly Sabbath	2nd Night
Saturday Day		2nd Day
Saturday Night		3rd Night
Sunday Morning	Resurrection	3rd Day
It was the first day of the week that Jesus was resurrected, (Matthew 28:1).		

The Sheaf of First Fruits (Leviticus 23:10)

This sheaf corresponds to Jesus the first begotten of the dead, the acceptable one before the Father, who is the herald of the harvest to come (Revelation 1:5). As such he ascended to the Father after completing the work so that the in-gathering may occur (John 20:17).

The New Meal Offering (Leviticus 23:15-16).

This feast, fifty days after the wave sheaf of first fruits, we now know as Pentecost. It was on this day the Spirit of God was poured out upon the people of God and the church began its work to go into all the world. The harvest had begun (Acts 2:1-4). Indeed, the Church, which started at Pentecost, is described as having the first fruits of the Spirit (Romans 8:23).

The Feast of Trumpets (Leviticus 23:23)

The blowing of the trumpet corresponds to the return of the Lord when His Church will be caught up to meet Him in the air. The Rapture will manifest firstly with the sound of the trumpet (1 Thessalonians 4:16, 17).

The Day of Atonement (Leviticus 23:27)

The Day of Atonement was a day of mourning and confession of sin. This feast corresponds to the Nation of Israel acknowledging their Messiah as Jesus, (Zechariah 12:9-14). At that time Israel will be received as a cleansed nation by their Messiah (Zechariah 13:1).

The Feast of Tabernacles (Leviticus 23:34)

The Feast of Tabernacles was the celebratory feast after the harvest. It speaks of the Millennium and beyond when the Lord harvests the crops of humanity, and we will all enter our rest. It has however particular significance for Israel in the Millennium (Zechariah 14:16-18).

Different Interpretations

There are many different ways in which people have interpreted Revelation. Different beliefs have been proposed by those who are genuinely Christian. They have loved the Bible and have been diligent to study the scriptures to form the conclusions they have had. They have also been sincere in the opinions they have held.

In briefly surveying these points of view readers must study the book for themselves and decide which point of view they accept. We must be careful to disagree with other opinions respectfully and lovingly. There should be no place for pride or unkindness in our debate with others regarding the book of Revelation. It is important we come to our clear conclusions firmly held but not invalidating the integrity of others who we may vehemently disagree with at times.

Contemporary Historical-Critical Approach

This approach is an attempt to view the text within its own historical, social, political, cultural and intellectual setting (Harding, 2015, pp. 12-13). The Historical-Critical Approach has been very much an approach favoured by some academics from the mid-nineteenth century to the present day. It is an attempt to isolate the text in its own time to keep a historical-critical distance. It can lead to conclusions which many believe are non-traditional and indeed unbiblical.

For example, some authors following this approach would conclude that two writers wrote Revelation and it was compiled by a third. This method is inconsistent with the belief that the book of Revelation is one book written by one author and exactly word for word. The historical-critical approach is by definition critical and discounts the supernatural.

Historicist or Church Historical Approach

The approach functions on the belief that the book of Revelation is an outline of the history of the world from the start of Christianity until the end of time. Many of the visions and descriptions therefore in the book of Revelation are viewed as having already occurred. The identity of the antichrist, for example, is considered to be a historical figure, e.g., Napoleon or Hitler. It accepts a literal, physical second coming of Jesus.

The schemes of interpretation within this approach have changed as time has moved on, as more events of history have taken place. There is also a tendency for some of the statements of Revelation to be played down in the historical happenings that they are said to symbolise. For example, currently it is hard to find an example from history when all the living in the sea dies. Some of these schemes have led writers to predict when the second coming will happen. The year-day principle has led to some calculations that anticipate the return of Christ. Not only is this unbiblical but estimates have changed when they have proven to be wrong with the passage of time.

This approach, some would contend, was unknown to the early church but first appeared in the middle of the twelfth century and was systematised by the Abbot Joachim. Many Protestant Churches tended to use this system applying the antichrist passages to the Pope and equating some of the Revelation passages to the Roman Catholic Church.

Preterist Approach

Preterists believe that Revelation is applicable only to the early church. They would say that the primary use of the book was in helping Christians in those days through the trouble they were experiencing. There is therefore little in the book, in the Preterists view, for the church today. It was as a whole scheme taught by the Jesuit Alcasar published in 1614. It limits the scope of Revelation to the events of the Apostle John's life and affirms that the prophecy referred to the destruction of Jerusalem by Titus in AD 70.

Idealist Approach

The Idealist Approach is also known as the Triumphalist or Symbolic interpretation. The emphasis is that the book of Revelation contains moral and spiritual principles which apply to every age. They would say the whole book is symbolic and the contents are not actual events. In other words, it emphasises the symbolic but denies the literal in the book.

Futurist Approach

The Futurist viewpoint centres on the declaration in Revelation (Revelation 1:19) that parts of the book are in the past, parts are in the present and parts are in the future. It allows for a literal interpretation but acknowledges the symbolic aspects of the work. Futurists believe that the bulk of Revelation from (Revelation 4:1) is in the future. Futurism has become the dominant interpretive approach within the church during the last century. It is on this interpretive basis that I will be writing about the Book of Revelation.

However, there has been an attempt to marry this method with present-day events to evoke an expectation that the Second Coming is about to happen which brought the approach into some disrepute when over a period of a few years predictions did not occur. Futurists, not surprisingly, would argue that this has been the oldest approach that the church followed when interpreting Revelation but would acknowledge, that in its current form, it dates from modern times.

Introducing John

As a young man, together with his brother James, John met Jesus at the Sea of Galilee where he worked as a fisherman. This meeting happened around A.D. 30, though probably slightly earlier than this. He wrote Revelation towards the end of the first century A.D., and he would have been an old man at this point. In writing about himself in the gospel of John he comes across as a gentle, mild-mannered and self-effacing individual. He does not refer to himself by name but rather as the disciple whom Jesus loved.

There was, however, another side to him as demonstrated when he wanted to call down fire on some Samaritans who would not receive Jesus. Again, during his time with Jesus, he did not look kindly on some groups who were not part of his team (Mark 9:38). It is not surprising as a disciple with his brother James they earned the nickname 'Sons of Thunder.' When he grew older he was intolerant to falsehood but increasingly loving to people. In his writings, he uses the words for love eighty times. Jesus entrusted to him the care of his mother when He was dying on the cross (John 19:26).

John worked tirelessly for others through the years and became a leader of the churches in Asia Minor. Unlike Luke, he was not as educated as some, yet he wrote five books of the Bible. These include John's Gospel and three letters known as 1 John, 2 John and 3 John. His final book was called Revelation. His writings in some ways are simple in structure and vocabulary but profound in what they contain. It is much easier translating John's writings than Luke's from Common Greek because Luke wrote imitating a Classical Greek style. John was targeted as an old man by the Romans for being a Christian leader.

The Roman authorities banished him to Patmos, an island just off the coast of Asia Minor, where he had to work in the mines. At this time of banishment and suffering he had a marvellous visitation from Jesus. He saw visions of what would happen in the end times. John then wrote to the churches that he served, and so the book of Revelation came into our Bibles. He died approximately in A.D. 98.

Often Christians who are facing intense persecution experience Jesus drawing near to them in extraordinary ways. Many of these Christians, after these times of persecution, say that although they don't miss the suffering, they do lose this particular sense of Jesus being near them.

Four Hundred and Ninety Years

There are four periods of 490 years associated with the nation of Israel. Each one of these periods displays a breach or break (parenthesis) because of sin or unbelief (Bullinger, 1975, pp. 5, 6).

From the birth of Abraham to the Exodus was 505 years. But the birth of Ishmael because of Abrams natural attempt to fulfil the promise delayed things by 15 years. 505−15=490.

From the Exodus to the foundation of the Solomon's Temple was 573 years. However, deducting the years of captivities because of Israel's idolatry, we get 573−93=480. To this, we need to add ten years to the work of completing and furnishing it up to the dedication of the temple, i.e., 480+10=490.

From the dedication of Solomon's Temple unto Nehemiah's return is 560 years. From this, we must deduct the 70 years captivity in Babylon, 560−70=490.

From Nehemiah's return to the cutting off of Messiah is 483 years. We are now living in the parenthesis caused by Israel's rejection of their Messiah. There remain seven more years.

Practically we see that unbelief and disobedience cannot thwart the purposes of God but does at times create a delay. It is a good idea that we seek to believe and obey God in the way we live our lives. Somethings may have delayed because of what we have done or thought that is wrong.

Seven World Judgements

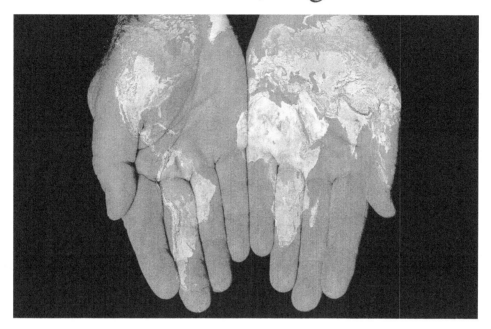

In the history of the earth, there are seven judgments from God involving men which are worldwide in scope. After each of these world judgments, life on earth has or will be considerably different. Some of these judgments have yet to take place. The implication of this is that we cannot infer how things will be in one of these periods by how things are now. These differences make visualising future events in the book of Revelation more difficult.

The significant world judgments are:

Adam in the Garden of Eden (Genesis 3)

When Adam sinned, death came upon the whole of the earth (1 Corinthians 15:22). People had to toil for their daily bread (Genesis 3:19).

The Flood (Genesis 6-8)

In the days of Noah God sent a flood destroying all humanity except for eight people. After this deluge the rain cycle as we know it became Gods way of watering the earth. Before this, a mist soaked the land (Genesis 2:6). God at this point also gave animal meat for people to eat (Genesis 9:3). God established the principle that murderers should have their blood shed by men (Genesis 9:6) but before this time murder was not punishable by death. Consider God's sentence on Cain when he was exiled rather than executed (Genesis 4:12).

The Scattering of Mankind at Babel, (Genesis 11)

After the flood humanity rebelled against the command from God to fill the earth (Genesis 9:1, 7). People planned to stay together and make a name for themselves (Genesis 11:4). God's judgment involved confusing the language of men and scattering them upon different parts of the earth (Genesis 11:1, 8). The nations speaking different languages only came into being at this time.

Jesus Dying on the Cross (Ephesians 2)

When Jesus died on the cross, He took the judgment of God for the sins of the world (John 3:16). His death has made the way for forgiveness for all who will put their trust in Him. Since the cross, grace rather than judgment has become available to whoever chooses to believe in Jesus (John 1:17). This world judgment of sin upon Jesus is in the middle of the seven world judgments.

The Second Coming (Revelation 19)

When Jesus returns, there will be a time of judgment. Strictly speaking, this begins with the seven-year period of Tribulation which precedes His return and culminates in the destruction of His enemies at Armageddon (Revelation 19:17-21). At this time, also the living nations will be judged when Jesus will separate the sheep from the goats (Matthew 25:32). Thus, at this critical point in earth's history, we see a sustained series of judgments which is reshaping the earth in preparation for the Millennium, a thousand-year period when life will be beautiful on earth. We know for example that the animal kingdom will not devour one another (Isaiah 11:6) and the deserts will bloom (Isaiah 35:1, 2).

The Judgement of the Rebellious Nations (Revelation 20)

Despite the favourable conditions on earth during the Millennium, there will occur another rebellion led by Satan at the end of the thousand years which results in fire coming down from heaven to burn up these rebels (Revelation 20:8, 9). The change that will be ushered in by this will begin with the dissolving of the creation as we know it by fire (2 Peter 3:7).

The Great White Throne Judgement (Revelation 20)

The Great White Throne is the final judgment of the resurrected who did not turn to Jesus for salvation. God will cast them into the Lake of Fire forever (Revelation 20:15). Following this judgment, there is a new creation and an eternal state where all who put their trust in Jesus will dwell in great happiness forever (Revelation 21:4).

Judgement is God's mechanism for affecting change. Without judgment, there would be no real change. People cry out for a change from the ongoing conditions of this fallen world. What we have to realise is that we are also crying out for the judgment of God. It is important that we prepare for both the change that God will bring and for the judgment which is a doorway into something far better.

Revelation 1

Revelation 1

1. The Revelation of Jesus Christ, which God gave to him to show his servants, what is necessary to arise quickly: and he signified it having sent it through his angel to his servant John: 2. Who witnessed to the word of God, and the testimony of Jesus Christ, as much as he saw. 3. Blessed is the one reading, and the ones hearing the words of the prophecy, and keeping the things having been written in it: for the time is near. 4. John to the seven assemblies in Asia: Grace to you, and peace, from the one being, and the one who was, and the one coming: and from the seven Spirits which are before his throne: 5. And from Jesus Christ, the faithful witness, the firstborn out of the dead, and the ruler of the kings of the earth. To the one having loved us and having washed us from our sins in his blood, 6. And he made us kings and priests to God and his father: to him be the glory and power into the ages of the ages. Amen. 7. Behold, he is coming with the clouds: and every eye will see him, even those who pierced him: and all the tribes of the earth will mourn over him. Yes, Amen. 8. I am the Alpha and the Omega, first and last, says the Lord, the one being, and the one who was, and the coming one, the Almighty. 9. I John, also your brother and participant in the trouble, and in the kingdom and endurance of Jesus Christ, was on the island called Patmos, because of the word of God, and the witness of Jesus Christ. 10. I was in the spirit in the Lord's day, and I heard behind me a great sound as a trumpet, 11. Saying, I am the Alpha and Omega, the first and the last: and, what you are seeing, write into a book, and send to the seven assemblies in Asia: to Ephesus, to Smyrna, to Pergamum, to Thyatira, to Sardis, to Philadelphia, and to Laodicea. (Revelation 1:1-11)

Prologue

Revelation is both a letter and a prophecy. As a letter, written to seven churches, it contains some information that is typical of most letters written both in the ancient world and in the modern. Our emails have the same information.

There are four key facts. These are the authors, the recipients, a summary of what the letter is about and an initial greeting.

The Author

The author of the letter is the Trinity - the Father, the Son and the Holy Spirit (Revelation 1:4) mediated by angels and written by John.

Jesus Receiving from the Father

Jesus received this Revelation from the Father (Revelation 1:1). Everything Jesus has He has received from the Father. Jesus has taken nothing for Himself by an independent act (John 17:1–5).

The Father has given to the son the testimony of the Father about the Son (1 John 5:9,10). He has authority to judge (John 5:27), miraculous works (John 5:36), the Church (John 10:29) and glory (John 17:22).

Jesus has taken nothing for Himself apart from what the Father has given Him. We should not presume, and appropriate things to ourselves not given us by the Father. Of course, the Father is very generous, and we should enjoy all His blessings. We should not be legalistic and poverty minded in our thinking about this.

Some examples of what we receive include the Spirit of God (1 John 4:13), His commands (1 John 4:21), eternal life (1 John 5:11) and understanding (1 John 5:20).

Jesus only did what he saw the Father doing (John 5:19). How many of our works have produced nothing because they were done from our imaginations rather than from God? It is essential that we learn to know from God what He has given to us and what He hasn't. We are not higher than Jesus in what we do.

The Father

The Father is, "Who is, who was and who is to come" (Revelation 1:4). The name of Jehovah is made up of three words meaning, "He will be, being and He was." Jesus' name is another form of the Hebrew name Joshua. Both mean Jehovah saves. So both in Jesus and the Father we see their eternal nature (Revelation 1:8).

The Holy Spirit

The seven Spirits refer to the Holy Spirit (Revelation 1:4). In the Old Testament Tabernacle, a seven-branched candlestick that shone upon a table of freshly baked bread (Exodus 25:31-39) depicted Him. The freshly baked bread was a picture of the Lord Jesus Christ (John 6:35), the Living Bread. The fact that the candlestick had seven branches reveals seven aspects of the work of the Holy Spirit (Isaiah 11:2). The Holy Spirit is:

The Spirit of the Lord (1) will rest on him, the Spirit of wisdom (2) and of understanding (3), the Spirit of counsel (4) and of might (5), the Spirit of the knowledge (6) and fear of the Lord (7)

So, there is only one Holy Spirit even though He is symbolised by seven qualities or attributes.

Angels and Symbols

Although Revelation has its origins in the Trinity, it was communicated a lot of the time though angels (Revelation 1:1). Angels feature more in the book of Revelation than any other book in the Bible. They are acting in their role as messengers again and again but also as the servants of God in judgment. They appear seventy-one times, that is twenty-five percent of the uses of the word in the Bible.

The way the angel made known the contents of Revelation was through the use of symbols. The word 'known' means signified. We use some symbols in our culture. An example of a symbol would be the colour red to signify danger or stop. In the time that John wrote Revelation symbolism was very common. People were very comfortable puzzling over symbols to come to an understanding of their meaning. It was considered disrespectful to tell people information in a direct manner. The implication was that if you were intelligent, you could work out teaching by deciphering the clues given in symbols. Also, people thought that learning through this process was better understood. It is a good principle that what we learn for ourselves we learn best.

Symbols are also a compelling way to teach what is beyond a learner's experience. Much of the content of Revelation is outside our experience. A picture or a symbol can very succinctly convey a significant amount of information. Try writing down a dream and its interpretation, and you will soon find it takes a long time to do this because of the amount of data generated.

The way we interpret the symbols used in the book of Revelation is to see how their usage occurs in other parts of the Bible. Comparing scriptures with scriptures decodes the symbols for us in Revelation. For example, John the Baptist tells us that Jesus is the Lamb of God who takes away the sins of the world (John 1:29, 36). We see the lamb spoken of as though slain (Revelation 5:6) thus we know this symbolises Jesus who died. Later we read of a beast that has two horns like a lamb (Revelation 13: 11) and we see a false Christ imitating the real Christ.

The word angel means messenger. The way this applies to angels in Revelation is significant.

There are three ways in which angels can figure in the book of Revelation:

1. There are the angels of the churches, which refer to human beings who act as messengers taking what John has written to the seven churches in Asia (Revelation 1:20).

2. Angels can refer to spiritual beings some good and some bad (Revelation 5:11, 12:7).

3. An angel can refer to Jesus (Revelation 8:3, 10:6). In both instances we see the messenger aspect of His ministry.

John, a Servant of God

John was the scribe who wrote down the letter (Revelation 1:11). In authoring this book we see the relation between the Trinity, ministering angels and the servants of God. When we are truly serving God, we are not acting either independently or without support. Service of God is always so supported even when we feel we are on our own (Acts 27:23, 24).

How is a faithful servant of God's teaching different from everybody else? Many people teach all sorts of things; some are helpful some are not. What is the best possible lesson a Christian can offer to others? There are two things that a Christian can teach that are the very best that others can hear. The first is the written word of God. The Bible is the Word of God. As such, there is no other book as authoritative or able to change people and their situations for good (Hebrews 4:12). For Christians to accurately teach others about the Bible, they must read and study this for themselves (2 Timothy 2:15). Part of this process is to also put into practice what they have read (James 1:22). There can be no clear ongoing understanding of the Bible apart from a willingness to do what God says in His Word (Mark 4:24, 25).

The second great thing a Christian must tell others about is the living Word of God (John 1:1). In other words, we should always be seeking to inform others about Jesus. Part of this testimony must again be the way we live. Because Jesus is not currently physically seen on earth, we as the body of Christ can demonstrate who He is to others. Jesus is the light of the world (John 9:5). He also calls Christians to be the light (Matthew 5:14). When Jesus taught others, He both did works and spoke (Acts 1:1). Moreover, the doing was before the speaking. We should do what we teach. A hypocrite is someone who does something different from what they say. The word hypocrite means to act like a performer in a drama. We are to avoid hypocrisy, (1 Peter 2:1). There are two things to avoid; doing but not speaking or speaking but not doing. There are many who in the name of witnessing for Jesus do good works but never talk about Jesus. How is this different from other people who do good but do not believe in Jesus?

In the Spirit on the Lord's Day

John was in the Spirit on the Lord's Day (Revelation 1:10). There has been a lot of controversy about this statement. There are two main views. The first is that the Lord's Day is a Sunday, the resurrection day of Jesus. The second is that John, when he was in the Spirit was transported to the Day of the Lord. Commentators also argue that the Greek from which 'Lord's Day' is from is not the common Greek phrase for the Day of the Lord.

I believe that John was taken in the Spirit to the actual Day of the Lord for the following reasons: -

1. Sunday is referred as the Lord's day nowhere in the New Testament Scriptures. The Bible, on the other hand, has a lot to say about the Day of the Lord.

2. Regarding the point about the unexpected Greek construction, it is by no means a clear argument that the phrase excludes the Day of the Lord (Pember, 1887, p. 328).

3. The Day of the Lord deals with a future time when God judges the world. It makes sense that John would be taken there to see visions of what is taking place.

4. The point of being in the Spirit is often overlooked by commentators who have never experienced this. It can mean being somewhere else (Ezekiel 11:24).

5. John is taken in the Spirit to the future even into a heavenly realm in (Revelation 4:2). Thus, time and space John transcended in the Spirit.

The Recipients

These were the servants of God and the seven churches in Asia.

The Servants of God

Revelation is to inform the servants of God what would take place (Revelation 1:1). The word servant here is better-translated service with the idea of bondage. The concept of a slave with a good master is perhaps in better keeping with the situation of the bondservant in this context. A bondservant was in a humble position. Also, there were some bondservants who under the law could go free after six years of service (Exodus 21:2-6). Some of these servants chose to remain as servants to their masters. A sign of this was pierced ears. We are to be bondservants of Jesus who humbly serve Him willingly not under any compulsion from the law. Pierced ears picture those who hear and obey. So, a faithful bondservant of Jesus obeys His commands. These are the qualities that are the key that unlock people's understanding of the book of Revelation. Those who live obediently and humbly following Jesus will understand the book and its contents. Those who do not, no matter how intellectually able they are, will not comprehend.

The Seven Churches of Asia

More specifically the letter was first addressed to seven churches in Asia. Asia does not refer to the continent of Asia nor even the area known as Asia Minor. Asia here was a region of the Roman empire that we would now think of as Turkey. The word church means an assembly. The Greek word is ekklesia. We get our English word ecclesiastic from this. The ekklesia were assemblies of people called out of towns and villages who met to make decisions about their towns or villages. So, the idea of the church being an ekklesia is an assembly of people who have been called out of the world to follow Jesus (Romans 1:7). These groupings were a mixed gathering of people some of whom were Christian but others who were only nominally so. They were, therefore, a mixture of the genuine and the false. The church does not refer to a building or an organisation but an assembly of people.

A Summary of What the Letter is About

The letter is about what John has seen, what is and what will take place (Revelation 1:19). The bulk of the book is looking at future events, but there are short accounts of what was and what is. The majority of the first three chapters look at past and present. Also, some parts of chapter 12 look at what has happened. The majority of the book of Revelation being a prophecy is future looking. 'Prophecy' starts with a preposition 'pro' meaning before. The word for prophecy means 'to say before.' Revelation, the prophecy, focuses on Jesus who is the fundamental focus of prophecy.

An Initial Greeting

The greeting is, "Grace and Peace." Grace is the undeserved kindness of God. Christians need not fear the coming judgment of God upon the Earth. God's attitude to us is one of undeserved compassion and peace (Romans 8:15). Christians should not fear to read the book of Revelation for God will save them from the coming anger that He is pouring out in judgment. The church will not pass through the seven-year period known as the Tribulation. They will not have to face the terrible time of the end.

Jesus Revealed

The last book of the Bible starts with the words, "This is the Revelation of Jesus Christ," (Revelation 1:1).

The way a book in the Bible starts provides the key to understanding. For example, the book of Isaiah begins with, "The vision of Isaiah, the son of Amoz, which he saw concerning Judah and Jerusalem" (Isaiah 1:1). From this, we see that much of Isaiah's prophecies came as the result of visions he had. The focus of these is particularly around the land of Judah and the city of Jerusalem. Isaiah tells us that the applications of these prophecies centre on Jesus, the Messiah, and the Jewish nation. Many have tried to apply Isaiah's prophecies to the church. A problem with this is that the promises of Isaiah are cherry picked for the church, but the curses are either ignored or applied to the Jewish nation. Such an application leads to a very inconsistent and faulty way of interpreting the book. Of course, there is much in Isaiah that is of great help and profit to the church.

Another example would be the book of Genesis which starts, "In the beginning" (Genesis 1:1). Genesis is very much the book of beginnings. It has been called the seedbed of the Bible. All the teachings of the Bible are in seed form in this book.

The last book of the Bible is a book which reveals Jesus. The word for revelation is Ἀποκάλυψις, pronounced apokalupsis which is why Revelation is sometimes called the Apocalypse. The word means to uncover. It is hardly surprising then that Revelation tells the story of God unveiling Jesus to the world.

When Jesus lived on earth two thousand years ago He was seen by some, mainly by His people, i.e., the Jewish nation (John 1:14). Of the Jewish nation, his disciples notably witnessed who Jesus is (John 2:11). During His time on earth, much of who He is Jesus hid. The King of glory humbled himself, took upon Himself the form of a servant (Philippians 2:7-8). At one point a little of that hidden beauty was revealed in what is known as the Transfiguration (Matthew 17:2). The Transfiguration was however only witnessed by three of Jesus disciples. After His death and resurrection, Jesus ascended high above all heavens to the highest place possible (Acts 1:9). His Ascension means that He is not usually now seen with physical eyes. At this time, Christians believe by faith, and there is a blessing for those who receive Him not having seen (John 20:29). At His return He will be witnessed by all (2 Timothy 4:1), (Revelation 1:7).

Revelation is a prophecy (Revelation 1:3). The nature of prophecy is that it testifies to Jesus (Revelation 19:10). The testimony of Jesus is the spirit of prophecy. So Revelation is all about Jesus and tells the story of how God reveals Him to the world. Revelation 1 is full of details about Jesus. He is not seen as the humbled servant but as the glorified Lord. These features are in two forms. Some are direct statements, others are in a figurative language. The power of the symbolic is that it enables the expression of the indescribable. The figurative language also allows a great deal of information to be very succinctly stated. A picture is worth a thousand words.

Jesus Described

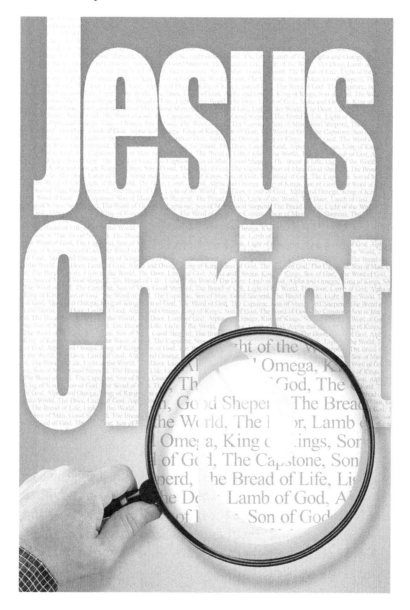

Literal statements about Jesus include:

Jesus Christ (Revelation 1:5)

The name Jesus Christ conveys a significant amount of information.

Jesus was named by Mary and Joseph at God's command through the angel that announced His conception through the Holy Spirit to Joseph (Matthew 1:21). The name of Jesus was given at this point because He would save His people from their sins. Jesus is another form of the name Joshua. Joshua means Jehovah saves. Again, in the name of Jesus we see Him linked to Jehovah. The Father and the Son are both of the Trinity. Jesus is God as is the Father.

Christ means the anointed one. Anointing refers to the act of putting oil on a person. There were three groups of people in particular who experienced anointing. Kings had an anointing (1 Samuel 16:1), priests were also anointed (Leviticus 6:20) and finally prophets (Zechariah 4:14). Jesus is the Prophet (Deuteronomy 18:18, 19), He is the Great High Priest (Hebrews 4:14) and King of kings (Revelation 17:14). Oil is an emblem of the Holy Spirit. Jesus has been given the Spirit without measure (John 3:34). The father has anointed the Son in a more excellent way than any other (Hebrews 1:9).

The faithful witness (Revelation 1:5)

When Jesus lived on earth, He witnessed to the truth (John 18:37). Jesus was a witness who was faithful unto death, (Romans 5:8).

The word martyr means witness. The context of the book is that of the persecution of John for being a Christian and his exile to the Isle of Patmos (Revelation 1:9). The Island was not used for this before the Roman Emperor Domitian came to power. Domitian (died 96 A.D.) was the first emperor to punish with banishment to the mines and quarries on Patmos which gives us some idea when John wrote the book. The theme of suffering for being a faithful witness runs throughout the book of Revelation. Right at the start, Jesus identifies with all His people who are loyal witnesses and suffering because of this.

Firstborn of the dead (Revelation 1:5)

In every way, Jesus is the first. He is the firstborn. In Bible times the firstborn was the honoured son who received the double portion of the inheritance. Jesus is the one who was the first man to rise from the dead and never die again. The First One has gone before and awaits us (Colossians 1:18). The word translated firstborn does not refer to a sequence of time but first in pre-eminence.

Prince of the kings of the earth (Revelation 1:5)

Every principality and power must be subject to Him. He is their Lord and Master no matter how much the wicked rage and plot against the truth and the people of God. Jesus ruling should be of great comfort to us that no matter what happens in our lives Jesus is in control (Philippians 2:9-11).

Loved us (Revelation 1:5)

How good it is to know that the Lord Jesus Christ loves us. Love for us motivates everything He does. We, the church, are the Bride of Christ (Ephesians 5:25). We should love Him in return and give Him everything we have got (Matthew 22:37). Whatever we do for God and others this commandment is the starting point.

Washed us in His own blood (Revelation 1:5)

The blood of Jesus cleanses Christians. It was necessary for His bloodshed to remove sin from believers. There is no other way we can be forgiven (1 John 1:7). It is crucial for us to remember the reason why we have our sins forgiven. We should not live with a sense of condemnation since the reason we received forgiveness is not because of us but through the death and resurrection of Jesus.

Made us kings and priests (Revelation 1:6)

Every Christian is a priest, not just some. Every Christian has authority to rule and not just some. Religion would promote some and reduce others. However, the church of Christ is not a hierarchy. It is a body (1 Peter 2:9).

The chief functions of a priest were to sacrifice (Leviticus 3:5), to teach (Deuteronomy 33:10), to intercede for others (Numbers 16:48) and to make judgments (Leviticus 13:3). A Christian is to offer up sacrifices of praise (Hebrews 13:15). We do not make sacrifices for the forgiveness of sins. In point of fact the Old Testament priests could not do that either (Hebrews 10:1). Only Jesus has offered a valid sacrifice for the forgiveness of sins and that once (Hebrews 10:12). We are to teach since that is part of the command Jesus gave to the church in proclaiming the Gospel (Matthew 28:20). We are to be people who pray for others (1 Timothy 2:8). We judge both now (1 Corinthians 2:15), and in the coming Kingdom (1 Corinthians 6:2).

To him be glory and dominion forever and ever. Amen (Revelation 1:6)

Jesus will reign forever and forever. He is currently sitting on the throne of the Father in the highest possible place (1 Corinthians 15:25). At this time, not everything is under His rule, under His feet (Hebrews 2:8). Revelation tells the story of how all things become subject to Him. He is the living stone that smashes the image of Gentile rule and makes it into dust that is blown away (Daniel 2:44).

Coming in the clouds (Revelation 1:7)

Jesus is literally, physically going to return to this earth. We don't know when, but He will surely return. One generation living on this planet will see this happen and live through the events of Revelation. There have been many enthusiastic Christians who have believed their age was the one. We must live in anticipation of Jesus' return but not go beyond what God has revealed. God has not shown the timing of this, and we should not be tempted to misuse Revelation to predict (Acts 1:7-11). Nevertheless, the coming of Jesus should cause us to live with a sense of anticipation. We have to live in the light that one day we will bow before Him and give an account of our lives.

Every eye shall see Him (Revelation 1:7)

Jesus' return will be the most obvious thing that has ever happened. He will not have to do a grand tour telling people He has returned (Luke 17:24).

Pierced (Revelation 1:7)

When men crucified Jesus, they pierced His hands and His feet. Moreover, they thrust a spear into His side (Psalm 22:16). It is clear that after His resurrection the marks of this piercing were still evident (John 20:27). These wounds are still apparent after His ascension and are shown in (Revelation 5:6). His love for us is demonstrated in His body even now.

The earth will wail because of Him (Revelation 1:7)

We must not think that because Jesus did not come to judge the world when he lived here on earth that His return will be on the same basis. His coming will bring joy to those who love Him but judgment and sorrow to those who reject Him. We do not help anyone by portraying Jesus as meek and mild. Men and women must prepare to meet Him while there is still grace and forgiveness offered to anyone who will believe in Him. Much of Revelation is dealing with a different season, a season of judgment and not grace. We must all stand before God and face judgment. Those who have placed their trust in Jesus and have received forgiveness of sins in this season will not have to fear the coming season (Revelation 6:15-17).

Alpha and Omega (Revelation 1:11)

Alpha is the first letter of the Greek alphabet and omega is the last. The book of Revelation was originally written in Common Greek which we now call New Testament Greek. Jesus is the first and last since Creation came by Him (John 1:3). He will renew Creation (2 Peter 3:10). Jesus is also the beginner and finisher of every Christian's faith (Hebrews 12:2).

Looking at the first and last letter of the Hebrew alphabet brings something more. Hebrew rabbis would speak of 'from aleph to tau' when talking about completeness or entirety. Every Hebrew alphabet letter had a meaning. Aleph stands for an ox and tau represents a cross. Biblically the ox represents the perfect servant (Psalm 144:14), (1 Corinthians 9:9) and the cross speaks of, Jesus' sacrifice (Hebrews 12:12). We are completely saved through the perfection of Jesus' service to the Father when He died upon the cross.

Jesus Seen

12. And I turned to see the voice which was speaking with me. And having turned I saw seven golden lampstands: 13. And in the middle of the seven lampstands one like the Son of man, having put on a foot-length robe and having been bound with a girdle to the breasts with a golden waistband. 14. But his head and hairs were white as white wool, white as snow: and his eyes as a blade of a flashing sword of fire: 15. And his feet like fine bronze, as having been set on fire in a furnace: and his voice as the sound of many waters. 16. Having in his right hand seven stars: and coming out of his mouth a sharp two-edged sword: and his face as the sun shining in his power. 17. And when I saw him, I fell to his feet like a dead man. And he placed his right hand upon me, saying to me, Do not fear: I am the first and the last: 18. And the one living, I became dead, and behold, I am living into the ages of the ages, Amen: I have the keys to Hades and Death. 19. Write the things you saw, and the things which are, and the things about to be after these: 20. The mystery of the seven stars which you saw upon my right hand, and the seven golden lampstands. The seven stars are the angels of the seven assemblies: and the seven lampstands are the seven assemblies. (Revelation 1:12-20)

The figurative vision of Jesus features:

Standing in the middle of seven golden candlesticks (Revelation 1:13)

The lampstands are the seven churches (Revelation 1:20). These churches were in Asia. The Asia Minor of Bible times is modern Turkey that we know today. The word Asia means 'mire' or 'slimy bog' (Tatford, 1947, p. 27). Asia is a picture of the church of Jesus Christ being in the world. The world is just like a slimy bog. It can suck people down and cover them in filth. The church's job is to shine a light on Jesus so that people can see Him.

We are also to bring light to people in danger of being destroyed by the wickedness of the world (Matthew 5:16). What an extraordinary privilege that Jesus, the all-glorious one, calls us to illuminate Him to a dark world! We only shine the light He has given us. The moon has no illumination of its own, but it can shine with dazzling brightness on a cloudy night because it reflects the light of the sun. As we reflect the light of the Lord Jesus, we can shine.

The lamps on the candlesticks were not candles but were little oil lamps. As such, they needed attending to keep shining. Jesus' walking in the midst of the lights indicates that He visits His people that they may continue shining and following Him (1Peter 1:5). There is also a responsibility on us to maintain our lamps. By that, I mean our walk with God. In the days of Eli, the priest, the oil lamps in the Tabernacle were allowed to go out (1 Samuel 3:2-3). Eli was an example of a careless priest. We as priests are to be not like this but diligent in our on-going walk with the Lord.

He wears a long garment down to His feet (Revelation 1:13)

Manual workers in Bible times did not wear long clothing. If they did, they had to tie the bottom of them up which people referred to as girding up their loins (Luke 12:37). Long clothes denote then a state of rest as opposed to work. Also, the rich wore long garments. In the East, a long robe was always a mark of honour and dignity.

When Jesus died on the cross, he finished His sacrificial work (John 19:30). In the Old Testament, the priests had no seats in the tabernacle or the temple indicating that their sacrifice continued. Jesus however as our High priest sat down because He has finished His work (Hebrews 10:12). Nothing more needs to be done for our salvation since Jesus has completed this. One priest who was often found sitting down on the job in the Old Testament was Eli (1 Samuel 1:9, 4:13, 18). God judged Eli for being unfaithful in his priesthood.

Wearing a golden belt about His chest (Revelation 1:13)

This kind of belt was used to carry money: it was hollow. All riches and treasure are in Jesus (John 3:35). The Old Testament high priest had a pouch over his chest containing two stones. One was called the "Urim" (meaning 'light'), and the other was called the "Thummim" (meaning 'perfection') (Exodus 28:30). What light and perfection are in Jesus. The way to receive real riches is to come to Him (John 6:68).

White hair (Revelation 1:14)

White hair revealed at this point directs the reader to (Daniel 7:9). One like unto the Son of Man stands before this white-haired figure and receives dominion, glory, and kingdom (Daniel 7:13, 14). God the Father is seen sitting upon His throne. He is the Ancient of Days. Jesus in this passage is the Son of man who is receiving dominion, glory, and kingdom from the Ancient of Days. Jesus with white hair in Revelation 1 is linking Him directly to the Father and is emphasising that both are God. It shows the eternal nature of Jesus. He is uncreated and has always been. It also foreshadows the events found in Revelation 4 and 5 where the Father gives unto the Son, dominion, glory, and a kingdom.

The Bible talks about those who have white hair (a hoary head). Those with white hair are people having a crown of glory, which has come about because they have lived righteously (Proverbs 16:31). White hair happens from living long, resulting from a life of righteousness. Jesus is the perfect man crowned with glory by the Father (Hebrews 1:8, 9). We need to aim to grow old following God. A life walked out with God leads to glory (Proverbs 4:18).

Burning eyes (Revelation 1:14)

Jesus is all seeing. Moses stood barefoot before the burning bush. All his ways were open and seen by the Lord (Exodus 3:5). The bare feet symbolise Moses ways were accessible and revealed to God. Seeing we will one day stand before the throne of God we should purify our ways of every evil and secret sin, (1 John 3:3).

Feet like burning brass (Revelation 1:15)

The word used for 'brass' refers to a golden like metal, if not more precious than gold. Feet are symbolic of the way someone lives their life, i.e., their path, for example (Proverbs 4:26, 27). The quality of Jesus' walk is very precious indeed (Romans 11:33). Our path is to be like Jesus. Such a life will also be beautiful and valuable in the sight of God (Song of Solomon 7:1).

Another aspect of brass is that it is used to refer to bronze used in military weapons. We begin to see Jesus as the judge of the earth who will war against His enemies.

His voice like the sound of many waters (Revelation 1:15)

Jesus is the Word. He speaks the water of life that refreshes us in every way (John 7:37). We need to love His words (Psalm 1:2, 3).

A good picture of Biblical meditation is the picture of the cow chewing the cud. A cow is not very good at assimilating its food. Because of this, it has more than one stomach. Initially, it swallows the grass into the first stomach. Later it regurgitates the partially digested grass (cud) and chews it more. It then goes into another stomach. The process occurs more than once. There is a difference between receiving the grass and assimilating it and making it part of the cow.

As Christians, it is one thing to hear the Word of God, and it is another thing for that to become part of us and for us to put this into practice. We do this by chewing over the Word of God when we face different situations in life. Meditation results in our walk dividing from evil unto righteousness (Leviticus 11:2, 3).

Seven stars are in His right hand (Revelation 1:16)

The right hand is the side of the double blessing. When Israel blessed Ephraim, he crossed his hands so that his right hand was on Ephraim's head. Manasseh was the firstborn and should have got the double blessing, but Ephraim got this instead. Ephraim means double fruitfulness (Genesis 48:17, 18). Jesus holds the church in His right hand, and as such, it is abundantly blessed (Ephesians 1:3). In difficulty, Jesus holds us in His right hand (Psalm 18:35).

We must distinguish between the stars, which are the angels of the seven churches and the candlesticks, which are the seven churches (Revelation 1:20). If we take the word 'angels' here literally for the stars, we have a problem. How could John write a letter to angels, what is their postal address? The word angel means 'messenger.' It makes sense that for John to contact the seven churches, he would write to specific individuals within the churches who would act as messengers.

A sharp two-edged sword comes from His mouth (Revelation 1:16)

The word of God is keener than any double-edged sword (Hebrews 4:12). Every word proceeding from the mouth of Jesus is irresistible (1 Corinthians 15:25). We should, therefore, be confident in Him, (Romans 8:31).

His face shining like the sun in full strength (Revelation 1:16)

The favour of the Lord is like the sun shining on the people (Numbers 6:24-26). He looks upon us with great support and blessing (Malachi 4:2).

The Keys to Hades (Hell) and Death (Revelation 1:18)

Hell is a real place with a physical location. The word Hell is the English translation of the Greek word Hades. When Jesus died, he descended to the lower parts of the earth (Ephesians 4:9). Comparing these lower parts of the earth with a prophecy about Jesus not being left in Hades (Hell) (Psalm 16:10, Acts 2:31), we see that Hell is located within the core of the planet.

Jesus gives us further information about Hades with the story of the rich man and a beggar called Lazarus (Luke 16:23-26). Both the rich man and Lazarus died and went to Hades. Hell was a place in two parts. There was the part most people think of when they think of Hell, a place of torment. However, there was also a different part of Hades where Lazarus was being comforted. Between these two different sections was a tremendous impassable chasm to stop people moving from one region to the other. Therefore, before Jesus' resurrection, when the wicked died, they went to a place of torment in Hell. The righteous also went to Hell but to a part where they were comforted. Without the sacrifice of Jesus at Calvary, there were no means for people to enter Heaven.

In the three days when Jesus was dead, He descended into Hell. Speaking to the thief who was being crucified with him, Jesus promised that the thief would that very day be with Jesus in Paradise. Jesus was referring to that part of Hell were Old Testament believers were comforted (Luke 23:43). There is no contradiction with Jesus descending into Hell and also being with the thief in Paradise.

While Jesus was in Hell, he proclaimed His victory to the evil spirits imprisoned there (1 Peter 3:18-20). It would seem that there is also in Hell a section where fallen angels are imprisoned (Jude 1:6).

After Jesus' resurrection, he ascended and brought out of Hell those righteous believers, (Ephesians 4:8-10). In other words, He set free the captives. With the resurrection, Jesus took hold of the keys of Death and Hell and unlocked those in Paradise. We see more evidence of this when Jesus rose from the dead, and other dead saints were observed (Matthew 27:51-53). Currently, the section in hell where people were comforted is empty, but the part where people are tormented is still filling up (Isaiah 5:14).

Since Jesus took possession of the keys of Death and Hell, Christians who die go straight to be with the Lord (Philippians 1:21).

Revelation 2

Introducing the Seven Churches

We are living in the time of the first fruits of the Spirit (Romans 8:23). The offering of first fruits was the only offering accepted by God containing leaven (yeast) (Leviticus 23:17). The significance of leaven or yeast, as we would call it now, is that it is something that is fermenting, i.e., in a state of decay. It, therefore, symbolises evil (Mark 8:15).

Every Christian is accepted by God, even though they have leaven still within them. We continue to do wrong but are longing for the day when we will be made perfect by the Lord when we are with Him. The assemblies of Christians on earth we call the church reflect this mixture of good and evil (2 Corinthians 4:7).

To further complicate this is present, within the assemblies of true Christians, those who are false believers who claim to be something they are not. The Lord knows His church. He praises many things but also calls the church to repentance on other issues (Revelation 2:2, 9, 13, 19; 3:1, 8, 15).

In each of the seven churches, He did not reject His people because of their flaws. Nor should we, as Christians, reject our fellow believers because of their faults. Furthermore, we must not dismiss ourselves when we see our errors. God calls us to repentance, not rejection.

The seven churches give us a good overview of both the strengths and weaknesses of the assemblies of God's people. Any study can major on the strengths or the weaknesses of these churches.

It is worth noting that before Jesus rebukes His people, He praises and commends then where He can. In our dealings with others, we would do well to follow this example (Colossians 4:6).

The messages to the seven churches have four applications:

1. To the churches addressed

2. To all the churches of all time.

3. Personal, to him that has an ear to hear.

4. Prophetic, the spiritual history of the church.

Ephesus, The Church that Left its First Love

1. To the angel of the Ephesian assembly write: These things say the one holding the seven stars in his right hand, the one walking about in the middle of the seven golden lampstands: 2. I know your works, and your labour, and your endurance, and that you are not able to bear evil men: and you have tested the ones claiming to be apostles, and they are not, and you found them liars: 3. And you have carried, and have endurance, and because of my name, you have toiled and not become weary. 4. But I have this against you, that your first love you abandoned. 5. Remember therefore from where you have fallen, and repent, and do the first works: but if not, I am coming to you quickly, and I will remove your lampstand out of its place unless you repent. 6. But this you have, that you hate the works of the Nicolaitans, which I also hate. 7. The one having an ear let him hear what the Spirit says to the assemblies: To the conqueror, I will give to him to eat out of the tree of life which is in the middle of the paradise of God. (Revelation 2:1-7)

The City

Ephesus means 'desirable' and living in the city of Ephesus, and the church were both very desirable. There are churches in places were many Christians desire to live. Some Christians look at other areas and the churches that are in these and dream of leaving their locality and spending time where they judge real spiritual life is taking place.

Ephesus was the most important city in Asia Minor because the Roman governor lived there. It had a population of between 250,000 and 500,000. Most notably it was the main harbour for the whole region and was located three miles up the Cayster River. The river, like so many tidal estuaries, was prone to silting and it was a constant battle to prevent the harbour from becoming unusable. Ultimately the struggle against silting was lost, and Ephesus is now an inland village with a few cottages. Ephesus was also a routing centre for land travel with four major Roman roads converging on the city. As a religious centre, it was renowned because of the temple of Artemis (Diana) located in the town. Reputedly it was built in the city because her image had fallen out of heaven there. The temple was one of the seven wonders of the ancient world. As a religious centre, there was all the vileness of pagan worship in which temple prostitution flourished, and Ephesus also had a reputation for immorality.

The Church

The church in Ephesus had an impressive history in the few years it had existed.

Paul's friends and fellow workers were present at Ephesus in the early days of the church (Acts 18:18-19). Apollos an influential teacher, eloquent and mighty in the scriptures, came to Ephesus where Priscilla and Aquila explained to him the way of God more accurately (Acts 18:24-26). Paul ministered in the city briefly on what is known as his second missionary journey (Acts 18:19-21), but much more substantially on his third missionary journey (Acts 19).

Ephesus was the city where God performed unusual miracles through Paul (Acts 19:11). Paul spent over two years preaching in the town and the surrounding areas. It seems likely that the other six churches in Revelation 2 and 3 formed as a result of the missionary work from Ephesus (Acts 19:10). Such was the impact of the Gospel upon the city that a riot occurred started by the silversmiths who feared their trade in silver idols diminishing by the number of people becoming Christians. A staggering number of magic books ended up on a fire totalling 160 work-years in wages.

After Paul, Timothy then continued to reside and teach at Ephesus (1 Timothy 1:3). Other notable workers included Onesiphorus (2 Timothy 1:16, 18) and Tychicus (2 Timothy 4:12). Church history informs us the Apostle John spent some years towards the end of his life in Ephesus where we think he wrote three epistles 1 John, 2 John and 3 John. In the last two letters, John describes himself as the elder (2 John 1:1), (3 John 1:1).

Even the most desirable of places and churches are not without their challenges. Four decades had passed since the beginning of the church in the city to when John wrote this letter Revelation. Forty years in the Bible is one generation. The Children of Israel wandered in the desert while one generation replaced the previous disobedient generation (Numbers 32:13). There is a need for each generation to choose to follow God for themselves. It does not necessarily mean that a previous strong generation guarantees following strong groups (Judges 2:7, 10). Many churches have started strong but as time has gone on have experienced a spiritual erosion or entropy.

There was once a church built when the Spirit of God was moving powerfully. The members of the church placed a noticeboard outside the church which read, "We preach Christ and him crucified." Time past and the next generation replaced the previous. They were not as strong or focused on God as their fathers on Jesus. Weeds began to grow in front of the noticeboard. The sign now read, "We preach Christ." More time past and again a new generation replaced those in the church. The weeds grew further, and the only part of the sign which was left was, "We preach." Many Churches have been in existence for at least forty years. A new generation is arising. The challenge for them is to be as strong or even stronger in their following of God.

The Commendation

Despite the problems the church still had much to commend it. These included:

Good works (Revelation 2:2)
Our Christianity is to be faith combined with actions (James 2:26). As Christians, we will stand before the judgment seat of Christ. There what we have done will be tried by fire. We will receive a reward for those actions that stand the test. This judgment is not a judgment of sin since Jesus cleansed our wrongdoing on the cross. We do not fear punishment instead we seek to please the Lord and know His commendation (2 Corinthians 5:10).

Patience (Revelation 2:2)

Biblical patience means to continue despite great difficulty and pain to do what is right. The idea is to endure until the end. As Christians, we are to remain faithful to the Lord and His ways no matter what. There is a reward for this faithfulness (Hebrews 12:1, 2).

Cannot bear those who are evil (Revelation 2:6)

We are to love what God loves and to hate what God hates. We are to hate evil (Psalm 97:10). Moreover, we are not to help evil men to do evil works (2 John 1:10, 11). Nicolaitans were an example of people loving something that was evil. We do not know who these people were. However, we are to hate what God hates. The word means 'destruction of the people.' We need to hate anything that is destructive to us or others (Philippians 4:8). There are two opinions as to who the Nicolaitans were. Some people speculate from the root meaning of the word, 'nikao' (conquer) and 'laos' (people) that the Nicolaitans were a distinction increasingly made between church members and their leaders which we know as clergy and laity. They would argue that such a difference divides the people of God and exalts a small number of professional leaders (Grant, 1955, p. 31). Another group of people, citing Irenaeus, believe the Nicolaitans were a sect founded by Nicolas of Antioch, one of the deacons. They taught that since grace saved them, they could live without regard to morality. The cult practised every kind of immorality as the pagan culture around them.

Tried them which say they are apostles (Revelation 2:2)

The word 'tried' means to scrutinise or put to the test. The Bible condemns those who have a faulty balance for weighing goods (Proverbs 20:23). In other words, we are to be people who consider what we hear and see and make correct judgments about this. Such considerations include the claims made by people. The Bible condemns having a judgemental and critical attitude towards others which is not the same as seeing people and situations for what they are (Job 12:11). There are many people today who claim to be Apostles. We would do well to question closely how many of these are true apostles. Two noticeable features of apostleship often seem missing from many who make such claims. Miraculous signs accompany Apostleship (2 Corinthians 12:12) and much suffering (1 Corinthians 4:9-13). How many of those who claim to be apostles evidence these signs?

The Church Corrected

Despite all these good qualities many in the church left their first love (Revelation 2:4). King Solomon was an example of someone who was seduced into loving other gods because he married lots of foreign wives who followed other gods (1 Kings 11:4, 5). We must guard our hearts against the love of the things of this world (Proverbs 4:23).

They were commanded to repent (Revelation 2:5). We are not victims of what we love or don't love. We can change what we feel about something. We can choose to love what we don't like and decide to forsake what we do love; hence we can repent. Love is also a choice and an action which may or may not lead to the pleasant feelings we associate with love. To hear can either mean to listen or it can be to obey. So, he who has ears to hear let him hear, (Revelation 2:6), means if you have heard this obey what is said. It would appear the church as a whole failed to follow the word they heard. The lampstand of the church Jesus eventually removed, and the testimony of this group did not remain (Revelation 2:5).

Even if we move to a church in a place that has a reputation of spiritual life this does not mean that it will remain the church we were attracted to nor does it remove from us our responsibility to keep loving Jesus with all our hearts.

Smyrna, The Suffering Church

8. And to the angel of the assembly of Smyrna write: These things says the first and the last, who became dead and possessed life: 9. I know your works, trouble and poverty, (but you are rich), and the blasphemy of the ones designating themselves to be Jews and they are not, but a synagogue of Satan. 10. Fear nothing which you are about to suffer: behold, the devil is about to throw some of you into a prison, that you might be tested ten days: become faithful up to death, and I will give you the victors crown of life. 11. The one having an ear let him hear what the Spirit is saying to the assemblies: The one conquering will absolutely not be harmed by the second death. (Revelation 2:8-11)

The City

Smyrna comes from the word myrrh. Myrrh is a gum resin from a shrubby tree. This resin tastes bitter and is the root meaning of the name. Myrrh functioned as a perfume (Psalm 45:8). It was one of the ingredients of the anointing oil used by priests (Exodus 30:23). Women used it for purification (Esther 2:12). It was linked to suffering and death because people used it for embalming (John 19:39). Myrrh was also a painkiller (Mark 15:23).

Smyrna was a wealthy commercial city, some forty miles north of Ephesus. It was fiercely loyal to Rome, and the citizens took great pride in this. At the time, of this letter to the church in Smyrna, the city had become fanatical in its worship of the Roman emperor. Citizens were expected annually to sacrifice to the emperor. Under Domitian, it was a capital offence not to do this. When Christians refused, the authorities viewed them as politically rebellious.

Jesus Revealed

Jesus identifies Himself to the church as the one who died and came to life. He is reminding His people that as they are suffering, He also suffered. As the first and the last, he is also emphasising that he is in control of everything that is happening.

The Church Commended

Jesus commends the church for its faithfulness despite being under considerable pressure to compromise. Ironically Christians were labelled atheists because of their refusal to believe in the multitude of gods and goddesses that other people worshipped. As atheists, they were open to accusations of lawless living. Hostile, unbelieving Jews took advantage of this and levelled slander against the Smyrnean Christians. Residents accused Christians of cannibalism because of the observing of the Lord's Supper (1 Corinthians 12:23-26). People labelled Christians immoral since they greeted one another with a kiss (Romans 12:16). When married people became Christians, sometimes their spouses did not convert which could lead to the breakup of marriages (1 Corinthians 7:12-14), and this gave grounds for the accusation that Christianity destroyed family life.

It is the norm for Christians to face slander and persecution (2 Timothy 3:12). We should not be surprised when we experience this. It is important to realise that we must remain faithful to Jesus and not deny Him at this time (Matthew 16:24-26). It is helpful to remember that Jesus remained faithful when suffering because He kept His eyes on the joy that would result from this (Hebrews 12:2). There is an excellent reward for those who remain faithful when tested by persecution (James 1:12).

Smyrna is one of the two churches that Jesus does not correct. They were not without fault, but the Lord knows how to encourage and not overwhelm His people. He was not going to add to their sorrows and would not suffer additional burdens on them. He will never let us go beyond what with His help we can withstand (1 Corinthians 10:13).

A Promise

To be a Christian in Smyrna meant that it could cost a citizen their property, their freedom, and their life. He encourages the Smyrnean Christians to remember there is a special reward for faithfulness a crown of life and safety from the second death.

Pergamum, The Church that Tolerated Evil

12. To the angel of the assembly in Pergamum write: These things says the one having the sharp two-edged sword: 13. I know your works, and where you dwell, where the throne of Satan is: and you hold my name, and you have not denied my faith, even in the days when Antipas my faithful witness was killed among you, where Satan dwells. 14. But I have against you a few things, because you have there, ones holding the teaching of Balaam, who was teaching Balak to throw a stumbling block before the sons of Israel, to eat meat offered to idols, and to commit sexual immorality. 15. In this way, you have also ones holding the teaching of the Nicolaitans, which I hate. 16. Repent: but if not, I am coming to you quickly, and I will wage war with you with the sword of my mouth. 17. The one having an ear let him hear what the Spirit is saying to the assemblies: To the one conquering I will give to him to eat from the manna having been hidden, and I will give him a white stone, and upon the stone a new name having been written, which no one knows except the one receiving it. (Revelation 2:12-17)

The City

Pergamum was the ancient capital of Asia. For a long time, the Attalid kings had their palaces and thrones in this city. When Rome began to dominate the area, Eumenes II decided to ally himself with the growing empire. As early as 133 B. C. Attalus III bequeathed the kingdom in his will to Rome.

The city was not renowned for trade it was more a pagan cathedral city, a university town, and a royal residence. It had a reputation for learning and had a famous library, second only to Alexandria, which held 200,000 books. The use of parchment was perfected in Pergamum after Alexandria banned the supply of papyrus to the city because of its attempts to surpass Alexandria as the preeminent library. Vellum is a writing material based on animal skins and is more durable than papyrus. Our word 'parchment' is from the name Pergamum.

The city was also famed for its medical science. It had some impressive pagan temples for Zeus, Athene, and Apollo. Its most magnificent temple was to the god Aesculapius. Aesculapius was the god of medicine, also known as the 'saviour' and 'preserver.' His depiction was often as a serpent. People would travel to Pergamum seeking health. Many non-poisonous snakes inhabited the temple of the god Aesculapius. People seeking health would sleep in the temple hoping they would have the god visit them and heal them through the agency of these snakes.

Jesus Revealed

Jesus particularly highlights to the church that he has the sharp two-edged sword. He is reminding the assembly of two essential things.

The sharp two-edged sword is the Word of God (Hebrews 4:12). This Word is living and powerful and divides soul and spirit. God's Word will always separate what is natural from what is spiritual. The church needed to be reminded of this because they were merging the worldly with the godly. There was a great need to separate the precious from the vile (Jeremiah 15:9). We do this by obeying what God says in His Word.

The sword in Roman days was the highest order of official authority, and the Proconsul of Asia could use this. The right of the sword was the ability to decide life or death for people under the proconsul's rule. Jesus, therefore, is also portraying Himself to the church as the one who rules with all authority and who will judge the church and the world.

The Church Commended

Jesus commended the church for holding firmly to the name of Jesus and not denying His faith. They remained steadfast despite two things.

The first issue was they dwelt where Satan's throne was. Living in a city where the population honoured the serpent as the 'saviour' would have been a significant challenge. Another issue was an immense monument to Zeus which stood in the city. It was 100 feet square and 800 feet above the plain, the altar of Zeus. We live in an increasingly pagan society. As such it is more challenging to remain uncompromising in our Christianity and much more comfortable to conform to the ways of an unrighteous community that is all around us.

Pergamum was also the centre of Emperor worship. It was on this issue that the early church was most likely to be martyred. Once a year each member of the city would have been required to offer a sacrifice to the emperor. Failure to do so was an offence punishable by death. Many suffered death and torture on this issue. Antipas could well have suffered martyrdom because of this. Tradition has it that he died in a brazen bull that was heated until it was red hot. Discrimination and persecution are increasing in our society against Christians. It seems probable that this will intensify the more our nation turns away from the Word of God. The challenge will be to remain faithful and not deny the name of Jesus.

Every pagan temple had their temple prostitutes. It was part of idolatrous worship to commit fornication. Indeed, those who did were considered true worshippers. How quickly people call good evil and wrong good as a society turns away from the truths of God.

The Church Corrected

The church tolerated people who held to two false teachings. One had its roots in the Old Testament, the other in the New.

The teaching of Balaam was the first of these. Balaam was an ancient false prophet who had a reputation for cursing people. Balak, a Moabite king, hired him to curse the Children of Israel. Despite God telling Balaam, he should not go, his love of money meant that he went anyway. Three times Balaam tried to curse Israel and three times God brought words of blessing out of his mouth. Balaam still wanting money from Balak suggested a different way to harm the Israelites which involved using the Moabite women to seduce the Israelite men into sexual immorality and idolatry. As a result of these 24,000 men died.

There are still people motivated by money who Satan uses to bring harm upon Christians by seeking to seduce them with immorality and the worship of things. They seem so attractive but are ultimately very destructive. We should flee these and those who teach that it is alright to pursue them. We must not tolerate the false in the church (2 Peter 2:1-22).

The other teaching was the doctrine of the Nicolaitans. There are two views as to what this was. Some believe it was the distinction between clergy and laity that was coming into the church. Nicolaitan can mean 'rulers over people' (Ironside, 1919, p. 36). Jesus taught that he was the head of the church and that we are all brothers (Matthew 23:8-12). In other words, there is no place for hierarchies within the church. Others believe that Nicolaitans were an impure sect which indulged in extreme sexual immorality while claiming to be Christians. They so emphasised grace that they used it as an excuse to do whatever they wanted. Grace has freed us from the demands of God's law that we might willingly follow Jesus not that we might use this as an excuse to sin (Romans 7:4-6).

The central issue for the Church of Pergamum was not that they were doing these evil things but tolerating those who taught that it was acceptable to do them. Increasingly the toleration of evil people the world is presenting as a virtue in our culture, and frequently this is influencing people's thinking within the church. It is not right to tolerate what is wrong.

A Promise

God promises two things to those who overcome.

Jesus promises hidden manna. God gave manna to the Children of Israel in the desert. It was bread which came down from heaven and fed them as they journeyed. Some were placed in a pot and hidden in the Ark of the Covenant in the Tabernacle. Manna speaks of Jesus and the life that He gives to those who believe and follow Him (John 6:51). In other words, Jesus is promising Eternal Life to those who overcome.

Jesus also promises a white stone. The people of Pergamum would have recognised the symbolism for this. The city inhabitants would celebrate with white stones and mark days of calamity with black. In court, the signal for guilt was a black stone and a white stone for innocence. Victors received white stones in games. Regarding hospitality, stones were also given to close family friends with their names inscribed upon them which indicated a warm welcome would always be given to them when visiting. White stones were the ticket for people in the temples who intended to take part in the feasts. These stones had the secret name of the god, and this was known only to the holder of the stone.

Thyatira, The Church that Believed Lies

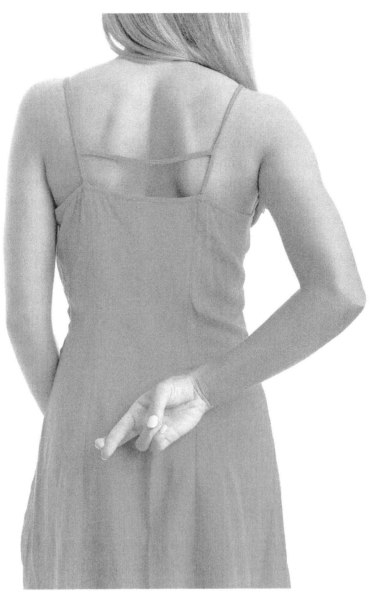

18. And to the angel of the assembly in Thyatira write: These things says the Son of God, the one having eyes as a blade of a flashing sword of fire, and his feet like fine bronze: 19. I know your works and love, and service, and faith, and your endurance, and your works: and the last is more than the first. 20. But I have a few things against you because you permit the woman Jezebel, the one calling herself a prophetess, to teach and lead astray my servants to commit sexual immorality and to eat meat offered to idols. 21. And I gave her a time that she might repent from her sexual immorality: and she did not repent. 22. Behold, I throw her into a bed, and the ones committing adultery with her into great trouble, unless they repent from their works. 23. And her children I will kill in death: and all the assemblies will know that I am the one searching minds and hearts: and I will give to each of you according to your works. 24. But I say to you, even to the ones remaining in Thyatira, as many as have not this teaching, and who knew not the depths of Satan, as they say: I cast no other weight upon you. 25. Nevertheless, what you have, take possession until I arrive. 26. And the one conquering, and the one guarding my works until the end, I will give to him authority over the nations: 27. And he will shepherd them with an iron sceptre: As the vessels made of clay are crushed: Even as I also received from my father. 28. And I will give to him the morning star. 29. The one having an ear let him hear what the Spirit is saying to the assemblies. (Revelation 2: 18-29)

The City

Thyatira was built as the first line of defence to protect Pergamum. It was on a relatively flat terrain and as such had no natural protection. The purpose was to slow down an enemy advancing on Pergamum. The city suffered many defeats and rebuilds. It came into a period of peace when the Romans conquered it in 190 B. C. Because it was on the main north-south road it prospered commercially under the Roman order. At the time of the letter written to the church, the city was very prosperous.

Thyatira's main industry involved dyeing materials with a purple dye. In Philippi, Paul met Lydia a seller of purple from Thyatira (Acts 16:14). Her conversion is the first reference we have of any Christians connected with the city. Because of the industrial nature of the town, there were many workers guilds. To work and trade in the city membership of the guilds was necessary. Each guild had an affiliation with a god and required its members to worship this god. This worship involved both eating food sacrificed to idols and also temple prostitution. Being a Christian in Thyatira was very challenging because of this.

The chief god of the city was Apollo, the sun god. He was also known as Tyrimnas. Worshippers represented him as a warrior riding forth to battle armed with a double-edged battle axe. Apollo was an appropriate city deity for a city that had been set up as a Macedonian military city guarding a pass.

Jesus Revealed

Jesus reveals himself very much as the advancing warrior to this city with flaming eyes and feet armoured in military burnished brass. He is showing the church that he is the real God of the town. Also, he is revealing himself as the one who comes warring against His enemies and fighting against those false believers in the church who are corrupting and leading His people to sin.

The Church Commended

Despite the challenging environment, many in the church lived godly lives. Four qualities were love, faith, service and patient endurance. Love has to be the foundation of all that we do. Whatever we do if unmotivated by love is worthless before God (1 Corinthians 13:1-3). Without faith, it is also impossible to please God (Hebrews 11:6). True faith displays good works. We are not saved by our works but by faith. For those who believe; God produces the fruit of good works in their lives (James 2:17-18). Service conveys the idea of working in a humble and menial way. We are to humble ourselves and become of no reputation in doing the work that God calls us to. Many promote themselves in the name of Christian service in our society. God loves the humble and the faithful (Philippians 2:5-8). A snowflake glorifies God by its hidden beauty even though most people never see its secret treasures (Job 38:22). Let us glorify God in secret, and he will one day reward us openly (Matthew 6:3-4). Not only did they work humbly motivated by love and faith, but they continued in these works. It is one thing to start well but another to end well. God wants us to finish well no matter how poorly we have begun or failed as we have gone along (Ecclesiastes 7:8).

The Church Corrected

There was a severe issue in the church of Thyatira that centred around a prophetess who Jesus symbolically referred to as Jezebel. Jezebel was an evil queen who married Ahab, a wicked king of Israel. She led Israel into the worship of Baal. This religion was vile and depraved. It involved sexual immorality and idolatry. Jezebel was also a murderess and had many false prophets working to promote the mistaken belief.

Many within the church had been influenced by this prophetesses' teaching and lured into sexual sin and idolatry. There were some teachings prevalent in the day that she could have used to do this. Philosophical dualism taught that the spirit was good, but the flesh was evil. It, therefore, followed that God was only interested in the spirit and what people did in the flesh didn't matter. Antinomianism means not law. This teaching argued that since grace saves us, we are not under law. People who believed this did whatever they wished no matter how contrary to God's law. Such teaching would have provided a false foundation for church members who were under pressure from the guilds to indulge in both idol worship and sexual immorality which would give them a rationalisation for combing these practices with a confession of Christian faith.

In our current churches, some members do in secret, and even now more openly things that are contrary to the Word of God. Some quite notable leaders are arguing that it is alright to do these things. Many are bowing to the pressure of society to embrace a compromised and polluted Christianity. The situation of the Thyatiran Church readily reflects much of what is our so-called Christianity.

Jesus is very strongly saying that He will judge His church. Judgement always begins with the house of God (1 Peter 4:17). We as Christians must return to the fear of the Lord. For the God who judged Ananias and Sapphira is still head of His church (Acts 5:1-11). He will be very zealous to finish the work He has begun in the Bride of Christ.

A Promise

Just as Jesus rules and reigns so will those who are faithful to obey Him at this time. There are a crown and a reward for those who remain committed to Him in difficult times and situations (2 Timothy 2:12). The faithful will receive the morning star which is none other than Jesus Himself (Revelation 22:16). If we have Christ, we have everything. Without Him no matter how much we have, we have nothing (Matthew 16:26).

Revelation 3

Sardis, The Church with a False Reputation

1. And to the angel of the assembly in Sardis write: These things say the one having the seven Spirits of God, and the seven stars: I know your works, that you have the name that you live, and you are dead. 2. Become watching and set fast the things remaining which are about to die: for I have not found your works having been fulfilled. 3. Remember therefore in what way you had received and heard, and guard it, and repent. If therefore you do not watch, I will come upon you as a thief, and you will definitely not recognise at what hour I will come upon you. 4. You have a few names even in Sardis, which have not defiled their clothes: and they will walk about with me in white: because they are worthy. 5. The one conquering, this one will be clothed in white garments: and I will absolutely not wipe out his name from the book of life, and I will confess his name before my Father, and before his angels. 6. The one having an ear, let him hear what the Spirit is saying to the assemblies. (Revelation 3:1-6)

The City

Sardis had an impressive history. It was one of the greatest capital cities of the ancient world. It was a city built on gold. Residents minted gold and silver coins there. Located near the royal road that led to the Persian capital of Susa it was on major trade routes. It was also a significant producer of garments and dyed products.

At first sight, the city seemed impregnable. The original town stood on a smooth nearly perpendicular rock with access only from one side. An extensive settlement grew at the foot of this citadel. An ancient saying which meant to do the impossible was, "to capture the Acropolis of Sardis."

However, despite the appearance of strength, the city was captured. The guards confident of the impregnability only guarded the one accessible side. The Citadel fell when enemies scaled the 'impregnable' rock. The Romans eventually took control of the city in 133 B.C. An earthquake destroyed the city in A.D. 17. With help from the Emperor, Tiberius, Sardis rose again, and the inhabitants built a temple to him. Cybele was the chief goddess worshipped also known as Artemis or Diana.

At the time of the writing of the letter to the church, the city was in decline. There was evidence of a faded glorious past.

Jesus Revealed

Jesus describes Himself to the church as the one who has the seven Spirits of God. The Holy Spirit is the one who breathes life upon the dead and dying. It is through His work that true spiritual awakening and revival comes (2 Corinthians 3:6). The church was in real need of renewed life and as such this feature is particularly relevant to their needs.

The Church Corrected

The church at Sardis had a reputation of spiritual life but was in fact dead. Just as the city had once the status of greatness and impregnability, but in reality, had been defeated and was in decline, so the church reflected this feature. How many churches in our land have great reputations? Our culture has become very skilful in marketing and public relations. Some churches work hard on the image they portray. Status can be very misleading. Individuals seek to promote how spiritual they are in different ways with ministers being careful to display publicly examples of how active their ministry is.

The key to spiritual life lies with the Holy Spirit. The way we encounter the Holy Spirit in our lives is to do as Jesus did. Jesus loved righteousness and hated wickedness, and because of this He was anointed (Hebrews 1:9). Many people are seeking to encounter the Holy Spirit. There has been a focus on external forms for doing this which without the real substance of a genuine walk with God is only an empty religious shell. We can spend hours 'worshipping' and 'fasting' and yet not encounter God. The music can stir emotions and give us a false sense of spiritual encounter, but the worship God seeks is in spirit and truth (John 4:23, 24).

There was a need for the church to wake up. Again, in the history of the city guards failed to protect the citadel. In the military practices of the day, an army officer would patrol to see if the sentries were awake keeping guard. If the officer found one sleeping, he would cut off part of the soldier's garments which would be used to confront him the next morning, and there would be punishment for dereliction of duty. In this sense, the officer came as a thief and the soldier's garments defiled.

Again, and again the Bible urges us to be watchful. We remain vigilant by judging ourselves from the Word of God and repenting where we see ourselves drawn into a compromise with either the ways of the world or failing to do what God has told us (1 Corinthians 11:31).

The Church Commended

The Church as a whole Jesus does not commend in this letter. There are some who are faithful and who have not defiled their garments. The city being a cloth dyeing centre would readily identify with this picture. Garments link to people's character in the Bible (Jude 1:23). So, within this church were those who were genuine and lived according to what they claimed to believe. We need to seek to be people who are both sincere and true in our faith (2 Timothy 1:5). The reputation and the practice need to match.

A Promise

In Roman festivals, the honoured guests wore white togas. Such people would walk in places of honour in the victory procession and feast afterwards in pure white garments. So, shall the people of God who are true Christians walk and feast with Christ at the wedding supper of the Lamb (Revelation 19:8, 9). Each city had a list of citizens. If a city member were found guilty of treason or disloyalty, the populace would blot their name out of the register and when a citizen did a particularly noble deed their name would be in gold on the citizen's scroll honouring them. Every true believer is in the citizen's register of heaven and fixed forever in this book.

Philadelphia, The Church with an Open Door

7. And to the angel of the assembly in Philadelphia write: These things say the holy, the true, the one having the key of David, the one opening and no one closes: and closes and no one opens: 8. I know your works: behold, I have given before you a door having been opened, and no one is able to close it: because you have little power and you have not denied my name. 9. Behold, I give from the synagogue of Satan the ones calling themselves to be Jews, and they are not, but they lie: I will make them come and bow before your feet, and they will know that I have loved you. 10. Because you have kept the word of my endurance, I also will keep you out of the hour of trial, about to come upon the whole world, to try the ones dwelling upon the earth. 11. Behold, I come quickly: grasp what you have, that no one may take your victors crown. 12. The one conquering, I will make him a pillar in the inner temple of my God, and he will definitely not go out again: and I will write upon him the name of my God, and the city of my God, the new Jerusalem, the city comes down out of heaven from my God, and I will write upon him my new name. 13. The one having an ear, let him hear what the Spirit is saying to the assemblies.
(Revelation 3:7-13)

The City

Attalus, king of Pergamum, built the city. Attalus had a brother called Eumenes to whom he was particularly loyal and devoted. Because of this, he was also named Philadelphus and the town named after this. Philadelphia means brotherly love.

The city was at a vital pass that led into the high central plateau of Asia Minor. The city was in effect an open doorway into the regions beyond. Philadelphia had the express purpose of spreading Greek culture and language in the eastern parts of Lydia and Phrygia. In that sense, it was very much a missionary city.

Philadelphia was much troubled by repeated earthquakes. The local population on some occasions abandoned their houses and lived in temporary accommodation outside the city.

Geographically brotherly love and an open-door link to the city.

Jesus Revealed

Jesus emphasises three things as He addresses this church. These are His holiness, His truth and that He has the key of David.

Only God is truly holy, and Jesus is demonstrating His deity by declaring this aspect of His nature (John 6:69). No one else is holy apart from the sanctifying work of God.

Jesus is the truth and every word He speaks we can fully trust (John 14:6).

Shebna, the treasurer, was removed and Eliakim took his place. God said of Eliakim that he would have the key of the house of David (Isaiah 22:15-22). Jesus now quotes these very words for Himself showing all government and treasure are in His hands.

In emphasising these three qualities, Jesus is laying a foundation for the commendation He is about to give the church.

The Commendation

Jesus praises the church for having little power, keeping Jesus' word and not denying His name. We are far weaker than we realise. Our strength is of God, and we are at our strongest when we recognise our weakness and put our trust in the Lord (2 Corinthians 12:9). Our culture portrays being strong and self-sufficient as something that is the norm and that such people are worthy of imitation. This attitude has also crept into the church. It is not normal to be self-reliant and self-sufficient. Most of the time we feel our weaknesses and are dependent upon others. Realising this brings humility and a kind attitude towards others who are weak. This church was in the place of brotherly love, and this is only possible when we have a balanced view of ourselves and others.

Keeping Jesus' words is essential. Obedience evidences our love for Him (John 14:21). Obedience leads to Holy living. We are pure in an impure world because we love our Saviour more than the desire of our fallen bodies to indulge in evil desires. Loving Jesus also empowers us to love others and is the foundation for the love of others. Loving others is the evidence that we truly love God (1 John 4:20).

The church did not deny His name. Demonstrating our love for one another is evidence that we are the disciples of Jesus (John 13:35). If we are too busy evangelising to care pastorally for one another, then we are undermining the very foundation on which we can efficiently proclaim the Gospel.

Jesus said nothing corrective to the Philadelphian Church. The church that truly loves one another is praised by God and knows the anointing of the Holy Spirit (Psalm 133).

A Promise

The church had an open door. An open door in the Bible refers to the opportunity to proclaim the Gospel (Colossians 4:3). We need to stop trying to emulate the latest evangelistic gimmick and return to loving God and loving one another. Love never fails (1 Corinthians 13)

Those who overcame would be pillars in the temple of God and would not go out. The columns in Solomon's Temple were called Jachin (establish) and Boaz (strength). God will establish and strengthen those saints who are like these Philadelphians. Moreover, they need fear no form of an earthquake. They will never have to leave the place of His presence and camp outside.

Laodicea, The Revolting Church

14. And to the angel of the assembly of the Laodiceans write: These things says the Amen, the faithful witness and true, the beginning of the creation of God: 15. I know your works that you are neither cold nor hot: I wish you were cold or hot. 16. Because you are lukewarm in this way, even neither cold nor hot, I am about to vomit you out of my mouth. 17. Because you say, I am rich, and I have become abundantly furnished with goods, and I have need of nothing: and you know not that you are wretched, and pitiable, and poor, and blind, and naked: 18. I advise you to buy from me gold having been purified out of fire that you might be rich: and white clothes that you might be clothed, and the shame of your nakedness not be laid bare: and eye salve to anoint your eyes, that you might see. 19. As many as I love, I reprove and discipline: be zealous therefore and repent. 20. Behold, I have stood upon the door, and I knock: if anyone hears my voice, and opens the door, I will come into him, and I will eat with him and he with me. 21. The one conquering, I will give to him to sit with me in my throne, as I also conquered, and I have sat with my Father in his throne. 22. The one having an ear, let him hear what the Spirit is saying to the assemblies. (Revelation 3:14-22)

The City

The inhabitants of the city were extremely self-reliant. They even refused help from Rome when rebuilding their city after an earthquake. They had great wealth and rebuilt boasting they needed nothing. Some of its wealth came from the quality of the black wool it sold. It also had a medical school renowned for its medicine especially ointments, in particular for the eyes. It was a centre for banking and people would exchange credit notes for gold in the city. The gold, however, had impurities in it.

Laodicea lacked a natural water supply. Water came from hot springs piped in from Hierapolis, six miles away, or cold water was brought down from the mountains. Either way, it was lukewarm when it reached Laodicea. The piped water was also full of sediment. All in all, the distasteful water was a downside to living in Laodicea.

The Church

Laodicea is the one church about which Jesus has nothing good to say. The church is so revolting to Him that he threatens to vomit them out of His mouth. The level of disgust expressed concerning this assembly is genuinely shocking. The members of this church who, having heard this criticism, did not repent could not possibly be genuine Christians even though they bore that name and assembled as a church. Those saved, Jesus He will never reject (John 6:37).

There were a number reasons why Jesus found this church so distasteful. Firstly, they said they were rich and had need of nothing. In this, they were expressing a reliance on self and worldly riches. It is the poor in spirit that is blessed (Matthew 5:3). True salvation is when we acknowledge our spiritual poverty and in our bankrupted state cry to God for mercy; putting our trust in Jesus (Psalm 49:7, 8). It was evident that these had a real love of money and possessions. It is not possible to love both God and money (Matthew 6:24). It is very tempting to trust in wealth rather than in God (1 Timothy 6:17). They were, therefore, attempting to occupy two mutually exclusive places at the same time which is the position the Israelites were in when they claimed to follow God but served the false god Baal. They were lukewarm, neither hot nor cold (Revelation 3:15). God particularly dislikes this (1 Kings 18:21). God wants our whole-hearted devotion.

There are some churches and Christians who are not genuine but are self-deceived. Jesus calls these to true repentance. He longs that He may indeed save them. They need to buy pure gold from Him. The Laodicean gold always had impurities, but the riches Christ offers is pure. Moreover, we buy without price and cost (Isaiah 55:1) which can happen because Jesus paid the price of redemption with His incorruptible blood when He died on the cross (1 Peter 1:18). The garments that Jesus offer to His people are pure white. He wants to clothe us in His righteousness (Isaiah 61:10). With salvation comes spiritual vision. We gain understanding through the work of the Holy Spirit who every true Christian has received (1 John 2:27).

A Promise

The well-known verse of Jesus standing at the door and knocking (Revelation 3:20) focuses on Christians, not unbelievers. Preachers frequently apply this in evangelism, and this is not a misuse of the scripture. We must not lose sight however of the context of the verse. God wants to sup with us. The supper was the main meal of the day. The idea is not that He comes in and feeds us instead we whole-heartedly serve Him. A great example of this is when the Lord appeared to Abraham in the heat of the day. This old man gave everything he had into serving the Lord. Abraham feasted and blessed the Lord, so should we (Genesis 18:1-8).

The Prophetic History of the Church

The letters suggest seven distinct periods, each with its peculiar characteristics, and it is significant to note that there have been seven such periods. Note the periods overlap to some extent, and that one does not necessarily cease before the next commences

Ephesus (Revelation 2:1-7)

Ephesus speaks of the church in the first century A.D. The love of the Christians is gradually waning in comparison to the first love and the faith in the Acts of the Apostles. Ephesus can be translated 'to let go or loosen.' Prophetically this corresponds to the first parable, the Parable of the Sower in (Matthew 13:1-7). The Gospel produces four different responses, not understanding, initial acceptance but turning away because of persecution, initial reaction but turning away because of the love of other things and fruitful whole-hearted commitment.

Smyrna (Revelation 2:8-11)

The Smyrnean period relates to the 250 years of the martyr period in which there were ten waves of persecution ending with the tenth persecution under Diocletian. Thousands of Christians died the death of martyrs. The name of the city means myrrh, an aromatic plant used in burials. Smyrna corresponds to the Parable of the Wheat and Tares (Matthew 13:24-30). In addition to this period being marked by great persecution, there was also a flood of false teaching and controversy. Indeed, all the significant errors connected with the church today have had their birth in this period. Tares were sown to grow up with the wheat.

Pergamos (Revelation 2:12-17)

The period depicted here is the church following the accession of Constantine. In A.D. 324 he adopted Christianity as the state religion and began to force it upon the empire. Pagan temples changed their names to Christian churches; pagan festivals converted into Christian ones. Pagan priests people labelled as Christian priests. Pergamos means twice married. Prophetically this corresponds to the Parable of the Mustard Seed (Matthew 13:31-32). In this parable, the birds of the air take shelter in the branches. So, paganism took up residence within the church.

Thyatira (Revelation 2:18-29)

Thyatira refers to the corruption within the church of the Middle Ages, with all its impurities, idolatries and persecutions, practising its wickedness, Jezebel like, under the cloak of religion. The name Thyatira means a continual sacrifice, which in essence is a description of the Mass which claims to continually offer up the actual blood and body of Christ every time celebrated. Prophetically this corresponds to the Parable of the Leaven (Matthew 13:33). The corruption that began to enter the church in Constantine's day reached a saturation point in the Middle Ages. Thus, the whole was leavened.

Sardis (Revelation 3:1-6)

Sardis describes the Reformation period of the church. As Sardis was accused of incomplete works so the Reformation while producing some excellent things, failed to purge the church of much that was pagan in its origins. The papal authority reformers limited and much truth in the Bible was restored. Protestantism increasingly became divided and soon became a lifeless religion. It started well but never came to fullness; it had an appearance of spiritual power but hid a weakness; it professed to have the life but was spiritually dead. Prophetically this corresponds to the Parable of the Treasure Hidden in a Field (Matthew 13:44). To have the treasure, people needed to buy the field. In other words, there was a treasure but mixed in with much wrong.

Philadelphia (Revelation 3:7-13)

The period represented here is the period of revivals including the Puritan, Methodist, Brethren, Pentecostal and Charismatic Awakenings. The worldwide missionary movements happened as depicted by the open door. Prophetically this corresponds to the Parable of the Pearl of Great Price (Matthew 13:45, 46). Many have given everything to God in these great movements.

Laodicea (Revelation 3:14-22)

Laodicea is the final state of the ecclesiastical structure before the Lord's return. This Church is a system that is increasingly ripe for domination and control by Satan. The true church is having to come out of this. Laodicea corresponds prophetically to the Parable of the Fishes (Matthew 13:47-50). There is a sifting of the good and the bad when the fishing net comes to shore, and God will sift the true church from the false at the time of Jesus' return.

Who is the Church?

Does it include the Old Testament Saints? What about those living in the Tribulation, are they part of the church?

The Holy Spirit and the Church

One essential element of being a Christian is having the Holy Spirit living within (Romans 8:9). The Holy Spirit is the guarantee of every Christian's salvation (Ephesians 1:13, 14). The church is the body of Christ, and we become part of it when Jesus baptises us into that body with the Holy Spirit (1 Corinthians 12:13). The idea of the word baptism is that of complete immersion and filling. It is a term connected to sunken ships.

Although the Holy Spirit moved in the Old Testament, He did not usually fill or indwell people. Most often He is spoken as coming upon someone for a specific time and purpose. An example of this was Samson (Judges 15:14). It was by this operation of the Spirit that Samson had great strength. However, when he failed to keep his vow as a Nazarite, the Spirit of the Lord departed from him, and he became weak (Judges 16:20). David, when he sinned against the Lord by committing adultery with Bathsheba and murdering her husband Uriah, was concerned that the Lord did not take His Spirit from Him (Psalm 51:11).

The Day of Pentecost changed everything when the Holy Spirit fell upon the disciples, and the church was born (Acts 2:1-4). Moreover, a Christian will never be in the place of losing the Holy Spirit any more than they can lose their salvation (John 16:7) and (1 John 2:27).

Old Testament Saints

On this basis then the Old Testament saints cannot be included in the church. They are saved and will be with Jesus forever through faith in Him, but their place in the works of God is different. The Old Testament saints had an earthly inheritance and earthly promises. Godliness for them on earth came with particular physical blessings including health and material prosperity (Leviticus 26:5-10).

A Heavenly People

The church is first and foremost a heavenly people with a spiritual inheritance (Ephesians 1:3, 2:6). In fact, we are pilgrims and strangers to this world (1 Peter 2:11). There was a distinction between Jew and Gentile, but in the church, this difference has gone (Ephesians 2:14). Our nationality is citizenship in heaven (Philippians 3:20).

The Mystery of the Church

The church was a mystery that manifested as the Jewish people rejected their Messiah. Initially, Jesus came proclaiming that the Kingdom of God was near. As time went on and repeatedly, the Jews rejected Him; His teaching began to change. When His disciples recognised and acknowledged that He was the Messiah, it was then that Jesus began to teach about the church (Matthew 16:18, 18:17). A mystery is something hidden until the time is right for its unveiling. Paul talks about this mystery as he teaches about the church (Ephesians 5:32).

Israel, the Church, and the Tribulation Saints

God made tremendous promises to the Jewish people that He will keep. However, when they rejected their Messiah things have been put on hold for them as a nation. Blindness in part has come upon the Israelites, (Romans 11:25). True many individual Jews believe in Jesus at this time and become part of the church, but the promises to the nation as a whole are on hold. We live in a parenthesis (gap) between the sixty-ninth and seventieth weeks of Daniel, (Daniel 9:24-27) which is Gods timetable for His dealing with Israel. The breach of promise has resulted in many blessings offered to the Gentiles, and many have benefitted with salvation.

We do not know how long this time will last but at some point, it will end, and the prophetic program for Israel will run its course. When that happens, the first thing Jesus will do is come for His Bride, the Church and will take her to His Father's house. As the prophetic clock runs its course Gods dealing will again be with Jews and Gentiles, not the church. The church is unmentioned on earth between Revelation 4-18 which deals with the remaining seven years before God's Kingdom is established upon earth. The Tribulation saints, while being the people of God, are not included in the church. We must not confuse the church with the godly people living through the Tribulation. They will fulfil a different calling in the plans of God.

The Restraint of the Holy Spirit

When the church leaves for heaven, the nature of the work of the Holy Spirit becomes different to what it is now. The restraining influence of the Holy Spirit will end, and much will then happen to the pain and injury of those dwelling on the earth. Currently, the Spirit reproves the world of sin, righteousness, and judgment (John 16:8). When the one who restrains functions in a different way the lawless one will come (2 Thessalonians 2:6-10).

Revelation 4

The Church Raptured from the Earth

1. After these things I saw, and behold, a door having been opened in the heaven: and the first voice which I heard as a trumpet speaking with me: saying, Come up here, and I will show you what is necessary to be after these things. (Revelation 4:1)

Revelation looks at what John has seen, what is now and what will take place later (Revelation 1:19). In Chapters 1-3, the past and present are primarily the focus. Chapters 4-22 mainly look at future events. (Revelation 4:1) begins with, "After these things," and ends with, "after these things." Verse 1 is emphasising that the book is now focussing on future events. But future events from which point? The churches, having featured so much in the first three chapters, are not mentioned again until (Revelation 22:16), which is the conclusion of the book. This is remarkable given that the letter was directly addressed to the churches.

So where have the churches gone 'after these things?' Enoch was a godly man who lived before the Flood. It was said of him that he walked with God but was not because God took him (Genesis 5:24). The New Testament supplies more information about this by telling us that God translated Enoch that he should not see death (Hebrews 11:5). Translate according to Vine means to move to another place, (Vine, 1973, p. 150). Enoch was moved by God from off the earth. Elijah a prophet was also translated not seeing death. We are told that a whirlwind took him up into heaven (2 Kings 2:1, 11). In the New Testament Jesus ascended from the Mount of Olives forty days after His resurrection, (Acts 1:9). Jesus is described as having been taken up.

Paul tells us that there is a day coming when the church will be caught up to be with Jesus (I Thessalonians 4:13-18). The Lord Jesus Christ will descend from heaven with a shout, and the voice of the archangel and with the trumpet call of God. The dead in Christ shall be resurrected and living Christians with them shall be caught up meeting the Lord in the air. This event is sometimes also called the Rapture. The word rapture is from 'rapere,' found in the expression "caught up" in the Latin translation of (1 Thessalonians 4:17). The church, therefore, is no longer on earth. The Rapture is excellent news for Christians in the light of what the world will face before the return of Jesus to the Mount of Olives. This is why Paul tells Christians to comfort one another with the truth of the Rapture. There is nothing for the Church to fear in the book of Revelation.

The Apostle is caught up into heaven, and this demonstrates the removal of the church into heaven. We are told that John was told to come up. It was not merely a vision but something he experienced. The Rapture is the first future event that will take place (1 Thessalonians 4:13-18). The trumpet is a feature of the church's removal from the earth. We know that the last trumpet sounds, (1 Corinthians 15:51, 52). This trumpet should not be confused with the last of the seven trumpets in (Revelation 11:15). The 'last trumpet' was a signal to move on from soldiers' encampments. A horn sounded for the nation of Israel when travelling through the desert (Numbers 10:6) and also for Roman soldiers when moving on. There were a series of trumpet soundings telling the soldiers to prepare, assemble in ranks and finally to set out. The voice of Jesus, trumpet-like (Revelation 1:10), is going to call His church heavenward and that is what literally will happen.

The Government of God

The Mechanism of God's Rule on Earth

2. And immediately I became in spirit: and behold, a throne was being laid down in the heaven, and upon the throne, one sitting. (Revelation 4:2)

God is the total ruler and Lord of all. He rules in the kingdoms and affairs of men (Daniel 4:17, 25, 32, 34). It is one thing to know that God rules but the mechanisms of how this works in the world are another matter. In the Bible, we have glimpses of how this process operates. As so much of this is in the unseen spirit realms our knowledge of this is not too detailed (1 Corinthians 13:12).

There is a heavenly court or assise that makes decisions which impact and affect the world of men. Within this council of God, God is ruling over all, there are cherubim powerful spiritual beings mainly connected with the government of the earth, and there are others, spirits some of whom are good, and some of whom are bad. These creatures are known by different names in different parts of the Bible and include watchers, holy ones, elders, gods and can include angels but may not consist entirely of these.

There are sometimes when this council is revealed and seen in operation. Micaiah the prophet had a vision of the heavenly assise passing judgment on Ahab and his subsequent death (1 Kings 22:19-22). Job was the subject of conversations amongst this council on two separate occasions, (Job 1:6, 2:1). Nebuchadnezzar was also someone who faced judgment from this group which resulted in him being humbled because of his pride (Daniel 4:17).

God requires righteous judgments from the members of this assise and will judge those who fail in this responsibility. Psalm 82 gives us a glimpse of this aspect of things.

This council would appear to be still functioning as a mechanism of government at this time (Ephesians 6:10-17). This Council is the place where Satan accuses the people of God day and night (Revelation 12:10) and would also explain specific actions of Paul when he delivered people to Satan's discipline (1 Corinthians 5:5), (1 Timothy 1:20).

There is coming a day when this court will cease to function. Revelation 4 and 5 describes the time when this happens. Currently, Jesus sits on the throne of God. He ascended to the highest throne, the eternal throne of God which is before and outside of creation (Hebrews 1:3). This throne is higher than the dominions of the current ruling council (Ephesians 4:10).

Daniel 7 gives another account of what is happening in Revelation 4 and 5 and is a process that takes place in the heavenly realms.

13 "I saw in the night visions, and behold, there came with the clouds of the sky one like a son of man, and he came even to the ancient of days, and they brought him near before him. 14 Dominion was given him, and glory, and a kingdom, that all the peoples, nations, and languages should serve him. His dominion is an everlasting dominion, which will not pass away, and his kingdom that which will not be destroyed. (Daniel 7:13, 14) World English Bible

There must come the point when the Lord Jesus Christ arises from the place of rest on the eternal throne and descends to the heavenly realms and stands before this council (Revelation 5:6).

The significance of the crowns of the elders being cast down is the handing over of authority to the Lord Jesus Christ who will take up the direct responsibility of judging the earth. At this time, He is not bringing judgment upon the earth rather His servants proclaim grace and mercy to the world. However, when Christ stands the world will shake, and judgment will be poured out.

Arnold's History of the Roman Empire gives an example of the casting down of crowns. In A.D. 63 Tiridates, king of Armenia avoided war with the Romans by renouncing his diadem to Emperor Nero. The ceremony in which this happened involved Tiridates having laid his crown before an image of Nero (Lang, 1945, p. 113).

Part of the process of the replacing of this court involves the forcible removal of Satan and his Hosts from the heavenly realms in which this assise has operated (Revelation 12:7-12).

The good news is that after this court is replaced by Christ and His work of judgment done Christians will rule with Him in this place of authority. An aspect of the judgment comes to believers at that time (1 Corinthians 6:2, 3).

Heavenly Visions,

Revelation gives us a glimpse of the heavenly realms. Something happens in the heavens, and then we see it outworked on earth. The events on our planet have first arisen in heaven. To understand Chapters 4 and 5, we need to identify who each figure represents.

One Sat on the Throne

3. And the one sitting was like in appearance a jasper stone and a sardine stone (carnelian – a precious reddish stone): and a rainbow all around the throne, like in appearance made of emerald. (Revelation 4:3)

The one who sits on the throne is God the Father. The good news is that whatever happens God reigns and rules over all. It all begins with Him. What He has decreed then occurs in the heavenly realms, and finally, seen on earth (Daniel 4:32), which is both concerning the wicked as well as the righteous. God rules over all. The evil ones are still corrupt, and the godly are still righteous even under God's rule. It is like a good horseman riding a lame horse. The horse will ride lame even though the rider is an excellent horseman.

The one seated was likened unto a jasper and a sardine (sardius stone) (Revelation 4:3). God depicts His glory with a jasper stone (Revelation 21:11). The one sitting on the throne is shining with the glory of God. In the Old Testament, the high priest wore a pouch on his chest called the breastplate. Fixed to this were twelve precious stones. The first stone was the sardius, and the last was jasper (Exodus 28:17-20). God, the Father, is the first and the last just as the Son, Jesus is (Isaiah 44:6).

A rainbow is about the throne (Revelation 4:3). God is about to judge the earth. It is appropriate that the rainbow is present since He remembers His covenant to never judge the world again with a flood of water. The rainbow is the sign of God's covenant with Noah and the air-breathing animals of the world (Genesis 9:13-15). Revelation likens the rainbow to an emerald (Revelation 4:3). The emerald takes its name here from its distinctive green colour. Green in scripture symbolises life (Luke 23:31). The flood smothered all breathing things outside the ark and covered all green vegetation. Thus, we see in Gods future judgment upon the earth that seed time and the harvest will be preserved. The fear of conservationists, about the world ending in an ecological disaster, is un-Biblical (Genesis 8:22). We shall, however, see the earth reshaped through a series of catastrophic judgements in preparation for the reign of Christ upon earth.

The Seven Spirits of God

5. And out of the throne came lightnings and thunders and voices: and seven lamps of fire burning before the throne, which are the seven Spirits of God. (Revelation 4:5)

The seven Spirits of God is the Holy Spirit. As we have seen in (Revelation 1:4), the Holy Spirit is one spirit but has seven perfect attributes (Isaiah 11:2).

The Twenty-Four Elders

4. And all around the throne twenty-four thrones: and upon the thrones, I saw twenty-four elders sitting, having been clothed in white garments: and they had upon their heads golden victor's crowns. (Revelation 4:4)

These are the saints who have gone to be with the Lord in heaven. In the Old Testament temple, which is a picture of heaven, both the priests and the prophets ministered before the Lord according to a rota of twenty-four divisions (1Chronicles 24:7-19) and (1 Chronicles 25:1, 9-31). We have here, therefore, those who are prophets, priests and kings. Angels are not described as priests or kings even though they are heavenly messengers. The saints of God, Christians, are prophets, priests and kings. We see all three aspects of this in (1 Peter 2:9). The elders are also recorded as singing a song which states that they were redeemed to God by the blood of the Lamb (Revelation 5:9).

These elders are wearing crowns. This type of crown is a victory crown, which marked kings victorious in battle or the winners in public games. The twenty-four elders (Revelation 4:4), represent the church having been raptured into heaven at a point before the Tribulation begins. We know that it is after the Rapture because they are wearing victors' crowns. Now Paul talks of receiving his victory crown together with everyone else after the Lord appears (2 Timothy 4:8). If the twenty-four elders were saints who had died and gone to be with the Lord before the Rapture, they would not have received their crowns at that point.

Not only do these elders have crowns but they are clothed in white garments. When Christians stand before the Lord Jesus, there will be a point when they are judged. This judgement takes place before a judgement seat (Romans 14: 10-12, 2 Corinthians 5:10). It would appear they receive both the white garments and the crowns as part of this process. The white gowns speak of the righteous acts of the saints (Revelation 19:8). The judgement seat of Christ is not for punishment but reward (1 Corinthians 3:11-15). It would seem that the judgement seat of Christ takes place immediately after the Rapture but before this heavenly council.

Twenty-four here should be taken as literally twenty-four. Certain of these elders are later spoken of as having conversations with John as one individual to another (Revelation 5:5, 7:13). Elders by definition are connected with a larger group of people and can represent them. The office of an elder is meaningless apart from a group in which they function in this role. Numbers in Revelation need to be viewed literally.

The Four Beasts

6. And before the throne a sea made of glass, like crystal: and in the middle of the throne and in a circle around the throne four living beings full of eyes before and behind. 7. And the first living being was like a lion, and the second living being like a calf, and the third living being having the face as a man, and the fourth living being like a flying eagle. 8. And the four living beings each one having six wings around: and within they are full of eyes, and they do not have rest day and night, saying, Holy, holy, holy, the Almighty God, the one who was, the one being, and the one coming. (Revelation 4:6-8)

These are the cherubim. They appear in (Ezekiel 1:5, 6). They are immensely powerful beings who enact the governmental dealings of God on the earth. Every time they are mentioned in scripture some of their details are different which is because various aspects of their work are in view.

A fourfold description is used to describe the peoples of the earth in the book of Revelation which occurs seven times:

1. (Revelation 5:9) Out of every tribe and tongue and people and nation,

2. (Revelation 7:9) of all nations, tribes, peoples and tongues,

3. (Revelation 10:11) many peoples, nations, tongues and kings

4. (Revelation11:9) the peoples, tribes, tongues and nations

5. (Revelation 13:7) tribe, tongue and nations (and people)

6. (Revelation 14:6) to every nation, tribe, tongue and people

7. (Revelation 17:15) peoples, multitudes, nations and tongues

The number four is very much linked to the earth as the cherubim are. The living creatures are likened unto a lion, a calf, a man's face and an eagle respectively (Revelation 4:7). These four categories of earthly life that breathed were present in the ark at the time of the flood (Genesis 8:18, 19). The eagle is representative of the birds. The calf is representative of clean animals. The lion is representative of unclean animals. The face of a man is representative of Noah and his family.

It is clear that Satan, as Lucifer, was also a Cherub (Ezekiel 28:14). It is hardly surprising then as a being made to have a governmental function over the earth that Satan is so preoccupied with the world out of all God's creation.

The six wings also indicate that there is a composite picture including the Seraphim (Revelation 4:8). The Seraphim are powerful spiritual beings who bring the fire of God. The word Seraph means to burn, i.e., to consume as in judgment. We see them linked to the fire on God's altar in (Isaiah 6:6). Thus, we know God's governmental dealings with the earth are to be with the burning of His judgment.

9. And whenever the living beings give glory and honour and thanks to the one sitting upon the throne, to the one living into the ages of the ages, 10. the twenty-four elders will fall before the one sitting upon the throne and they fall down to worship the one living into the ages of the ages, and they throw their victors crowns before the throne, saying, 11. You are worthy, Lord, to receive the glory and the honour and the power: because you created all things, and because of your will they are, and they were created. (Revelation 4:9-11)

We must never forget that God is the creator of all things. It is only because of Him that we are (Acts 17:28). Not only has He created all things, but they continue to exist because God maintains them (Hebrews 1:3). This creation also means that all things belong to Him (Psalm 24:1). Satan has attempted to take possession of the earth for himself. He considers himself to rule over the earth. When he tempted Jesus, he offered the kingdoms of the world to him (Matthew 4:9). How arrogant and full of pride Satan is offering the world to the one who created and maintains it! The business of this heavenly council is to address this very issue. The kingdoms of this world legally are Christ's, and the events of the council are about to confirm this.

Revelation 5

1. And I saw upon the right hand of the one sitting upon the throne a book having been written within and behind, having been sealed with seven seals. (Revelation 5:1)

At the time John wrote, people were very familiar with seven sealed scrolls in many different contexts. Two of these were title deeds to land and royal warrants to rule over a kingdom.

Title Deeds

Seven sealed scrolls were well known to people of the Middle East in Bible times. They were deeds or contracts. The full contract would be written on the inner pages and sealed with seven seals. The content of the deal would be described briefly on the outside. They were marriage contracts, rental and lease agreements, the release of slaves, contract bills and bonds (Thomas, 1992, p. 378). Jeremiah gives an example of a sealed title deed scroll in (Jeremiah 32:11).

When Adam sinned in the garden of Eden, he handed over his right to rule the earth to Satan. Satan became the god of this world (2 Corinthians 4:4). Part of Satan's purpose in tempting Adam and Eve was to steal man's inheritance from them. Satan is a murderer and a thief (John 10:10).

When the Israelites came into the land of Canaan, they were each given an inheritance by God. They were not supposed to sell or give up their inheritance. Many Israelites over time lost their land. One reason was that they became poor and sold harvest rights to the property. They were allowed to lease their fields for a time. It was possible to redeem the land before the lease expired but only if the owner had sufficient money to buy back the land. Failing this a close member of the family could purchase the land (Leviticus 25:23-25).

Men have never been able to buy back what Satan took, we have never been able to pay the price to do this (Psalm 49:7-8). Jesus became a man thus becoming our close relative. He also was able to afford the redemption price. Because Jesus never sinned he was able to purchase fallen mankind and to redeem the earth. The cost of this was His blood which he shed on Calvary when he was crucified (1 Peter 1:18, 19).

Currently despite Jesus having paid the redemption price and triumphing over Satan the world is still possessed by Satan. He is like a squatter trespassing on property that does not belong to him. God is the ultimate owner of the world and all that is in it. We see Him holding the title deed (Revelation 5:1).

Royal Warrants

Under the Roman Empire, various territories or kingdoms were ruled over by local kings or Roman officials. They ruled because they were given the authority to do this by the Roman Emperor, Caesar. For these rulers to come into their kingdoms, they had to travel to Rome and receive a royal warrant which was a document proving their right to rule. The Herods ruled over the Israelite lands on behalf of Rome. Each one had to take the journey to Rome before they could rule.

After Jesus was resurrected, he ascended into heaven. There he will receive His royal warrant to rule from the Father. Jesus told a story to illustrate this about a nobleman.

The Parable of the Ten Minas

A nobleman went into a far country to receive a kingdom and return (Luke 19:12). Herod the Great (40 BC) and Archelaus (4 BC) both went to Rome to win their territory before returning to rule in Jerusalem. Jesus has gone to heaven to receive His kingdom (Hebrews 1:13, 2:8, 9). The context of the parable was that the Kingdom of God was not immediately appearing. The parable of the talents has some similarities to the parable of the minas (Matthew 25:14-30) but is not the same. They are teaching two different things. The talents explain about the eternal damnation of the wicked; The minas denote the judgment of the people of God for reward.

The Parable of the Talents	The Parable of the Minas
The unfaithful servant suffered eternal punishment (Matthew 25:30).	The unfaithful servant suffered loss but not rejection by the nobleman (Luke 19:24, 27).
The sums of money were large.	The sums of money were small.
The servants received different amounts.	The servants received the same amount.

The seven-sealed scroll that Jesus is receiving from the Father is the royal warrant to rule. The breaking of the seals is Jesus enacting what He has upon the earth.

The Kingdom of God

God has always intended that Jesus will reign over all the earth.

Adam's Rule

A step towards this was the creation of Adam and Eve. God invested in Adam and Eve world rule (Genesis 1:26). When Satan tempted Adam and Eve to sin the right of world rule was stolen from Adam and usurped by Satan (Luke 4:6). At the time of Adam's fall God promised that there would arise a seed of the woman who would crush the serpent's head, this was foretelling the coming of Jesus and the destruction of Satan (Genesis 3:15).

Jewish Rule

From the seed of the woman, God selected one-man Abraham through whom the genealogy of Jesus would come. Abraham's grandson Israel prophesied that the coming king would be of the tribe of Judah, one of his sons (Genesis 49:10). Thus, the nation of Israel developed and was established in the land of Israel. God chose a king who was David, again an ancestor of Jesus. When David ruled over the nation of Israel God made a covenant with him that his house and his kingdom would be forever (2 Samuel 7:16).

This promise is currently unfulfilled. All the promises of God will come to pass fully in God's time. Often with prophetic words, for a time, the opposite seems to be happening. Things seemed to be moving in the right direction when David's son Solomon reigned. However, Solomon sinned, and as a result, the Kingdom of Israel split into two. There then followed a series of Jewish kings who to a greater or lesser extent did not obey God.

Gentile Rule

The result was that the kingdom passed away from the Jewish nation and world rule came to series of Gentile kingdoms starting with Nebuchadnezzar king of Babylon (Daniel 2:37-38). World rule passed from the ancestors of Jesus into the Gentile world. After Babylon, the Medes and Persians ruled. The Greeks then replaced this empire and finally were overtaken by the Roman Empire.

Daniel's Seventy Weeks

God had not forgotten His promises and, at the time of the prophet Daniel, gave a timetable of how world rule would be taken from the Gentiles and given unto Jesus Christ (Daniel 9:24-27). The prophecy said that 70 weeks (of years) were determined for the Jewish people to complete the promise given to David, i.e., 490 years.

These seventy weeks are in three sections, and some parts fulfilled.

1. The prophecy fulfilment began in the days of Nehemiah, 445 B.C. with the city of Jerusalem rebuilt taking seven weeks (of years), i.e., 49 years.

2. 62 weeks (of years), i.e., 434 years then followed and brought us to the time when Jesus came to the Jewish people as their King riding into Jerusalem on a donkey. However, the Jewish people rejected their King and Messiah. The next part of the prophecy was fulfilled with Jesus' crucifixion, 'cut off' in the actual words of the prophecy.

3. Daniels prophecy left one week, i.e., seven years to be fulfilled for the Gentile rule to pass back to the Son of David. The final week has yet to run its course.

God suspended His dealings with Israel as a nation after the sixty-ninth week because they rejected their Messiah. One day God will start the prophetic timetable again, and there will be the final seven years that end in Jesus ruling over all the earth. We currently live in this gap, between the sixty-ninth and the seventieth week, sometimes called a parenthesis. This parenthesis is good news for us since salvation can come to all who believe both Jews and Gentiles.

Satan's World Ruler

There will come the point when our time ends. The church will be moved out of the earth (1 Thessalonians 4:13-18). The restraints on the Devil's activities in the world will finish, and he will select a man to rule. This man will be a dominant world ruler energised by Satan. Increasingly this rule will become more destructive and murderous as time goes on. This terrible time is the Tribulation. Things will become so severe that unless God intervenes no one will survive.

Jesus' Rule

Jesus will then return to the earth as King of kings (Revelation 19:16). He will rule on the planet for a thousand years (Revelation 20:6). At last the kingdom will come, and the will of God will be done on the earth as it is in heaven (Matthew 6:10).

Revelation is telling the story of the return of the Lord Jesus Christ and the establishment of His Kingdom upon the earth (2 Thessalonians 1:7). The Kingdom will only fully come with the presence of the King. The word kingdom (Basilea) denotes sovereignty. This sovereignty requires the residence of a sovereign or King. There can be no kingdom apart from a king (Bullinger, 1974, p. Appendix 112).

This aspect of the King returning to establish the kingdom is brought out in (Luke 19:11-27). Jesus tells a story of a man going to a far country to receive a kingdom. Jesus, having ascended, has gone into the heavens to be given the Kingdom from the Father. This concept of rulers receiving their royal warrant was very familiar to the Jewish people. For example, all the Herod family had to go to Rome to obtain authority to rule over Israel and the surrounding districts. Having returned with their royal authority, they could then reign.

The Need for the Kingdom to Come

In Revelation 4 and 5 we see Jesus receiving the mandate to rule from the Father in the form of the seven-sealed scroll. Later in Revelation, we observe Him returning to rule in His Kingdom. Thus, at this time not everything on earth is under His rule (Hebrews 1:13). Even the thief on the cross recognised this aspect of the kingdom referring to Jesus one day coming (Luke 23:42).

Increasingly within the church is the idea that we are setting up the Kingdom of God upon earth. The idea is that when this happens, the King will return. Biblically it has never been the mandate of the church to set up the kingdom of God upon the earth. It is the commission of the church to preach the Gospel and make disciples. Historically every attempt to set up the Kingdom of God by the church has become increasingly corrupt.

Examples of how bad these have been are the Crusades or the domination of the church by the state in the Reformation. People have been tortured and martyred in the name of establishing the Kingdom of God upon the earth. It is clear at the return of the Lord Jesus there will be a massive worldly kingdom that will try very hard to prevent Him establishing His Kingdom (Psalm 2).

Another Aspect of the Kingdom

Jesus coming is one of two aspects of the Kingdom of God. The Kingdom of God is within every Christian (Luke 17:20, 21). As such we are called to be salt and light within the world. We have a position of influence in the world causing people to glorify God (Matthew 5:13-16). The church is the body of Christ upon earth, and as such we can influence people around us (Ephesians 5:30).

People who are not Christians are members of the kingdom of Satan and, although blessed by the presence of Christians in the earth, can only become part of the Kingdom of God through salvation in the Lord Jesus Christ by believing the Gospel (Colossians 1:13). Good works are good but cannot in themselves create the Kingdom of God upon the earth. People's response to the Gospel can establish the Kingdom of God within them.

Because there are two aspects of the Kingdom, there are two outcomes to the way we see the promises of God outworked in our lives. For example, when we pray for healing, there are times when the Kingdom of God manifests upon earth, and we see people healed. At other times, we don't see this happening, so we understand the need for the Kingdom to come in its fullness. Within us is the ongoing cry for God's Kingdom to come.

The Reign of Jesus Upon the Earth Legally Ratified

2. And I saw a strong angel crying with a great voice, Who is worthy to open the book, and to lose its seals? 3. And no one was able in the heaven, or upon the earth, or under the earth, to open the book, or to see it. 4. And I was weeping much because no one was found worthy to open and to read the book or to see it. 5. And one out of the elders says to me, Weep not: behold, the Lion out of the tribe of Judah, the Root of David, has conquered, to open the book, and to lose the seven seals. 6. And I saw, and behold, in the middle of the throne and of the four living beings and in the middle of the elders, a lamb having stood as having been slain, having seven horns and seven eyes, which are the seven Spirits of God having been sent into all the earth. 7. And he came and had taken the book out of the right hand of the one sitting upon the throne.
(Revelation 5:2-7)

The Lion of the tribe of Judah (Revelation 5:5)

The lion is the Lord Jesus Christ. The seven-sealed scroll is the title deed to everything. The real thrust of Revelation 4 and 5 is to show us that the title deeds of the universe are delivered unto the Lord Jesus Christ. He is the one who has purchased the possession. The consequence of Him taking hold of the deeds is that everyone everywhere will speak words of blessing to the Lord which is the result of the Lord claiming His inheritance (Revelation 5:13).

Jesus is the lion who is of the tribe of Judah (Revelation 5:5). A lion is noted for its strength, (Judges 14:8) and Jesus is the almighty one (Revelation 1:8). Nothing can resist the power of a lion, and no one will be able to withstand Jesus when He returns to rule upon the earth. Jesus' anger like a roaring lion (Proverbs 19:12) will proclaim the day of vengeance of God (Isaiah 61:2). As such, the lion is a good symbol of this. Jesus is of the tribe of Judah by physical descent (Matthew 1:1, 2). A prophecy says that there would come a ruler from this tribe (Genesis 49:10) and Jesus is the fulfilment of this prophecy.

Jesus is the root of David (Revelation 5:5). Seemingly the royal line of David collapsed after the fall of Jerusalem before Nebuchadnezzar. The kingly line was like a dead tree in a desert land yet out of that apparent dead-end Jesus was a branch from that root but also its source (Isaiah 11:1,10). Jesus is the root out of dry ground (Isaiah 53:2). Jesus is both the descendant of David but also the origin of which David came. He is both David's Son and David's Lord (Matthew 22:42-46).

Jesus is a lamb standing as though He had been slain (Revelation 5:6). A slain lamb is a contradiction, how can a slaughtered lamb stand? Jesus is the lamb of God who takes away the sins of the world (John 1:29), and He did this by being led as a lamb to the slaughter upon the cross (Isaiah 53:7). As such He is the lamb slain. However, God has raised Him from the dead (Romans 6:9) and thus the lamb slain stands.

Jesus has seven horns and seven eyes (Revelation 5:6). Horns in the Bible speak of strength to rule and overcome enemies (1 Samuel 2:1). Seven is the number of perfect completeness. The work of God making the heavens was perfected and completed in seven days (Genesis 2:1, 2). In Jesus, there will be a perfect overcoming of all His enemies. He will be entirely exalted over all who would oppose Him (Hebrews 10:13). The Spirit of God is all seeing and in this function as the eyes of the Lord, nothing and no-one hide (Proverbs 15:3). Men will attempt to hide but will be unable to do so (Revelation 6:15,16).

The Universal Song of Praise

8. And when he had taken the book, the four living beings and the twenty-four elders fell before the lamb, each having harps, and filled golden bowls of incenses, which are the prayers of the holy ones. 9. And they are singing a new song saying, You are worthy to take the book, and to open its seals: because you were slain, and you purchased us to God in your blood out of every tribe and tongue and people and nation: 10. And you made us kings and priests to our God: and we will reign upon the earth. 11. And I saw and heard the voice of many angels all around the throne, and the living beings and the elders: and their number was myriads of myriads and thousands of thousands: 12. Speaking with a loud voice, Worthy is the Lamb the one having been slain to receive the power, and riches, and wisdom, and strength, and honour, and glory, and blessing. 13. And every creature who is in the heaven, and in the earth, and under the earth, and which is upon the sea, and all in them, I heard saying, to the one sitting upon the throne and to the Lamb the blessing, the honour, and the glory, and the power into the ages of the ages. 14. And the four living beings were saying, Amen. And the twenty-four elders fell and worshipped the one living into the ages of the ages. (Revelation 5:8-14)

When Jesus suffered upon the cross, He endured the pain because He kept in mind the joy that would occur from this (Hebrews 12:2). If we would stand under challenging circumstances, we should do as Jesus did and fix our eyes on the result of remaining faithful in the trial (Hebrews 10:32-35). The consequence of Jesus dying on the cross is the redemption of the people of God who are the offspring of Jesus (Isaiah 53:10).

God deals with the principle of death and resurrection upon this fallen earth. At first sight, when Jesus died upon the cross, the King had been rejected and the work of three years ministry defeated at a stroke. It was the resurrection from the dead that completely reversed this in an instant turning seeming defeat into victory (Romans 1:4). We should not judge our experiences before God deals with us in resurrection power. Our lives are like seeds that fall into the earth and die that much increase may come from the work and energy of God. Under challenging circumstances, it is tempting to think that our hope has gone, but in a moment God can and does ultimately reverse this (Ezekiel 37:11-13).

The day is going to come when Jesus entirely rules over this earth. At this time, not everything is under His feet (1 Corinthians 15:25). The day will come when everything and everyone will worship Him (Psalm 2:6-12). Here we see the Cherubim and Elders worshipping Him (Revelation 5:8), and the angels worshipping Him (Revelation 5:11). Every created being adores Him, and that includes all those who have rebelled against Him (Revelation 5:13). The end of this account of Chapter 5 looks to the result of Jesus taking the scroll with all bowing before Him (Philippians 2:9-11).

In other words, this section of Revelation jumps ahead beyond what needs to take place for every knee to bow and to confess that Jesus is Lord. It is directly linking the taking of the title deed and royal warrant to the outcome. The Lord Jesus will rule over all and there will be none who will dispute this. Satan will be evicted from his illegal occupation of the earth.

Revelation 6

The Tribulation is a seven-year period that will happen immediately before the return of Jesus to the earth. Tribulation is an old-fashioned word meaning trouble. These seven years will be the most troubling years the world has ever known (Matthew 24:21). We know it is seven years because a seven-year period was prophesied happening immediately before everlasting righteousness would come to the earth (Daniel 9:24). A ruler will make a treaty with the Jewish nation (Daniel 9:27). The treaty will be broken after three and a half years. An image of the ruler will be placed in a rebuilt temple in Jerusalem (Matthew 24:15). Jesus calls the first half of the time the 'beginning of sorrows' (Matthew 24:8). The second half of these seven years Jesus identifies as 'great tribulation' (Matthew 24:21). These two sections are referred to several times in Revelation by forty-two months (Revelation 11:2, 13:5), one thousand two hundred and sixty days (Revelation 11:3, 12:6), and a time, times and half a time (Revelation 12:14).

The bulk of Revelation is focussing on these seven years and particularly the judgements that God will send upon the earth. There are three sets of judgements. Each set of judgements contains seven different plagues. These sets of judgements are described as seals being broken on a scroll, trumpets being blown, and shallow bowls being poured out as if upon a sacrifice on an altar.

The seal judgements are mentioned first with the trumpet judgements happening within the seventh seal being broken. The bowl judgements are called the last judgements (Revelation 15:1) and appear to occur within the seventh trumpet judgement. The seventh trumpet is blown for an extended time as described, 'in the days the angel begins to blow' (Revelation 10:7). All three sets of judgements conclude at the same point with the return of Jesus to the earth.

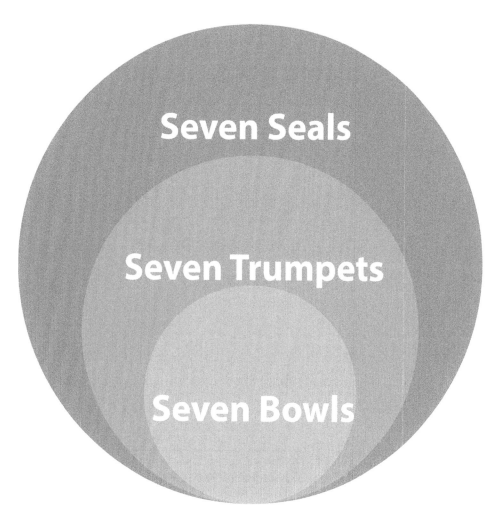

Many commentators have interpreted these plagues, seals, trumpets and bowls very figuratively. The prophecies that were fulfilled when Jesus came and lived on the earth had both a literal and spiritual fulfilment. It would seem more consistent with what has gone before to interpret these Tribulation judgements both literally and figuratively. Over spiritualising these events add to people's confusion about Revelation. Acknowledging a literal fulfilment and a basic chronological order within the text of Revelation makes the interpretation much simpler.

The Seal Judgements

Four Horses

The first four seals are horses with riders. The horse is the symbol of war (Job 39:19-25). All the aspects of war are revealed in the four riders and what results from this.

1st Seal

1. And I saw when the Lamb opened one of the seven seals, and I heard one of the four living beings saying, as with a voice of thunder, Come and see. 2. And I saw and behold a white horse: and the one sitting upon it having a bow: and a victor's crown was given to him: and he came out conquering, and that he might conquer. (Revelation 6:1,2)

The first rider is a conqueror with a bow riding on a white horse. In this seven-year period, there will be one who goes on a campaign of conquest. In the ancient world, the centaur was a half man and half horse carrying a bow always depicted without an arrow. The origins of this date back to Babel (Babylon) and the man associated with this namely Nimrod (Genesis 10:8-10) (Hislop, 1975, pp. 41, 42).

God described Nimrod as a mighty hunter before the Lord. The phrase 'mighty hunter' as translated in some versions, can be translated a mighty hunter of men. Man's rebellion after the flood centres around Nimrod. One of the reasons why Revelation has a lot to say about Babylon is that it gave the world its corrupt systems and structures that still permeate our lives. The conqueror who will come in the Tribulation will have all the characteristics of a rebel embracing a kingdom that is not of God (Daniel 8:23-25).

The white horse was the symbol of victory in the Roman Empire, and winners rode them in victory parades. So, we see this ruler being victorious in his conquests.

2nd Seal

3. And when he opened the second seal, I heard the second living being say, Come and see. 4. And another horse the colour of fire came out: and to the one sitting upon it was given to him to take the peace from the earth, and that they might slay one another: and there was given to him a great sword. (Revelation 6:3, 4)

The second rider denotes bloodshed with many killing each other. Red and blood are connected within the Bible, for example (Isaiah 63:2-3). So why is so much blood shed when Jesus judges the world? Much blood has been shed by men from Abel (Genesis 4:8-11) to the present time. Much more will be shed in the days to come. After the flood, God said that if man shed blood then by man his blood would be shed (Genesis 9:6). God has never rescinded this principle, and so we see the outworking of this in the time of judgement coming upon the earth.

3rd Seal

5. And when he opened the third seal, I heard the third living being say, Come and see. And I saw and behold a black horse: and the one sitting upon it having a balance scales in his hand. 6. And I heard a voice in the middle of the four living beings saying, A measure of grain for a denarius, and three measures of barley for a denarius: and the olive oil and the wine do not harm. (Revelation 6:5, 6)

The third rider is on a black horse. Black speaks of famine (Lamentations 5:10). Barley and wheat are basic foods, and these cost a day's pay necessary to buy a day's supply of wheat for one person. Oil and wine, luxury goods are not affected. Here we see food being rationed as denoted by the scales used for weighing.

4th Seal

7. And when he opened the fourth seal, I heard the voice of the fourth living being saying, Come and see. 8. And I saw and behold a pale green horse: and the one sitting upon it, the name for him Death, and Hades is following with him. And authority to kill the fourth of the earth was given with sword, and with famine, and with death, and by wild animals of the earth.
(Revelation 6:7-8)

The fourth rider denotes Death. Four things tend to go together. These are war, famine, disease and wild beasts. In the four riders, we have the four sore judgments of God upon the earth (Ezekiel 14:21). Zechariah also prophesies of these horses and riders (Zechariah 6:1-8).

Jesus commented explicitly on these four seal judgements when He answered His disciples' questions about the end of the world. He located these events during the beginning of sorrows in the earlier part of the Tribulation (Matthew 24:7, 8)

5th Seal

9. And when he opened the fifth seal, I saw under the altar the souls of the ones having been slain because of the word of God, and the witness which they were holding. 10. And they cried out with a great voice, saying, Until when, O Master, the holy one and true, do you not judge and avenge our blood from the ones dwelling upon the earth? 11. And for each of them were given white robes: and it was said to them that they should rest yet a little time, until their fellow servants and their brothers, the ones about to be killed as also they should be fulfilled.
(Revelation 6:9-11)

The fifth seal denotes all those martyred for the Lord. It is appropriate that they cry out for justice since this is the run-up to the Day of Judgement when the time of grace will end. They are not seeking to avenge themselves but are looking to God to do this, (Jeremiah 46:10). The blood of the martyred saints cries out before God as Abel's blood cried out, (Genesis 4:10). It is also clear from this seal that during this time many of God's faithful people will be martyred. Again, Jesus commented on this (Matthew 24:9-14).

6th Seal

12. And I saw when he opened the sixth seal, and behold, a great earthquake happened: and the sun became black as sackcloth made of hair, and the moon became as blood: 13. And the stars of heaven fell to the earth, as a fig tree throws its late figs being shaken by a great wind, 14. And heaven was swept aside as a book being rolled up: and every mountain and island were moved out of their places. 15. And the kings of the earth, and the preeminent, and the powerful, and the rich, and the commanders of thousands, and the powerful, and every servant, and every free hid themselves in the caves and in the rocks of the mountains: 16. And they say to the mountains and to the rocks, Fall upon us, and hide us from the face of the one sitting upon the throne, and from the anger of the Lamb: 17. Because the great day of his anger came: and who is able to stand? (Revelation 6:12-17)

A tremendous earthquake occurs when this seal breaks. All things will shake in the last days (Haggai 2:6, 7, Hebrews 12:26-27). Undoubtedly there will be both a physical manifestation and a spiritual shaking. This earthquake will not be like the earthquakes we experience from time to time upon the earth. This shaking will be of a far greater magnitude. It will cause every mountain and island to move. In other words, this is an earthquake that shakes the entire crust of the planet. Such a moving of the earth's crust could well cause the heavens to scroll like a book from the viewpoint of people upon the earth. God has caused the earth to stand still at one point in Joshua's day for twenty-four hours (Joshua 10:12-14). When Hezekiah was healed by God of his sickness, the earth moved backwards causing the shadows on the sundials to move backwards a number of degrees (Isaiah 38:8). At the end of this age, God is well able to move the earth's crust in such a way it causes the sky to scroll from the viewpoint of those upon the earth.

Similarly, both a spiritual and physical darkness will fall upon the earth (Joel 2:30-31; 3:15). The sun and moon and stars reveal signs and seasons (Genesis 1:14). When Jesus was born, the wise men were able to see from a star that He was born (Matthew 2:2). When Jesus died, the sun did not give its light for three hours (Matthew 27:45). Jesus tells us that the sun and moon will be affected during the Tribulation, (Matthew 24:29). He also warns of great spiritual deception at that time (Matthew 24:11).

The Gospel, God told in the stars, but the ancient world corrupted this. The reason why God hates astrology is that it is a corruption of the real Zodiac - The way of life (Bullinger, 1974, p. 19). The word for stars used in the Greek text can mean other heavenly bodies apart from actual stars. Meteors and meteorites would be included in this word. People are increasingly aware that planets have been struck by heavenly bodies. Many disaster movies have been made based on the earth being struck in this way. Revelation makes it clear that there will be a number of objects colliding with the earth during the Tribulation. The literal is a physical manifestation of the spiritual. The stars cast to earth denote spiritual principalities being driven out of the heavens and grounded upon the planet. Note that stars are used to speak of spiritual beings (Job 38:7). One of the terrible things about this seven-year period will be the increase in spirit manifestations upon the earth (Revelation 12:7-12).

There will come the point when wicked men realise the day of judgment has arrived and will be in terrifying fear of the Lord (Isaiah 2:19-21). Many will seek to hide in underground bunkers, mines and caves after this earthquake. Sadly, many will still not turn to God even realising this. Men will recover from their panic and continue in their wicked ways.

Revelation 7

1. And after these things, I saw four angels having stood on the four corners of the earth, holding the four winds of the earth, that the wind might not blow upon the earth, nor upon the sea, nor upon every tree. 2. And I saw another angel ascending from east of the sun, having a seal of the living God: and he cried with a great voice to the four angels, to whom it was given to harm the earth and the sea. 3. Saying, Do not hurt the earth, nor the sea, nor the trees, until we seal the servants of our God upon their foreheads. 4. And I heard the number of the ones having been sealed: one hundred and forty-four thousand out of each tribe of the sons of Israel. (Revelation 7:1-4)

The Parenthesis

There follows between the sixth and seventh seal a parenthesis. The purpose of this insertion, within all the judgment, is to give comfort and encouragement to God's people.

The four winds are held back until God's people are protected (Revelation 7:1).

God restrains wickedness until the time is right and He sets the bounds of this. We should never be afraid of the wicked (Hebrews 13:6).

The four winds correspond to spirits (Daniel 7:2).

The Bible links the presence of God to the east. In the Temple and the Tabernacle, the sanctuary, where the presence of God dwelt, was at the eastern end. Thus, the angel is ascending from the place of the presence of God (Numbers 3:38). Moving away from the east denotes and is linked with those who walk away from God (Genesis 3:24, 4:16, 13:11).

The earth is a picture of settled government (Jeremiah 49:36). It also speaks of the curse after the fall (Genesis 3:17-19). It is the place of the man of the earth who oppresses others (Psalm 10:18).

The sea is symbolic of nations and peoples in anarchy and confusion (Isaiah 57:20).

Trees are a picture of human pride and might (Daniel 4:10, 22).

Again, and again in Revelation we see wickedness restrained until God's time (2 Thessalonians 2:7). Nothing can come against us apart from God's will. And all things that go against us work for our good (Romans 8:28, 31, 32). No circumstance can separate us from His love (Romans 8:37-39). Every time Balaam tried to curse the Children of Israel God turned it into a blessing (Numbers 23:11). So, God turns every curse we face into a blessing.

Of those saved there are two groups the 144,000 of Israel and a great company of Gentiles.

1. The 144,000 of Israel

5. Of the tribe of Judah, twelve thousand having been sealed. Of the tribe of Reuben, twelve thousand having been sealed. Of the tribe of Gad, twelve thousand having been sealed. 6. Of the tribe of Asher, twelve thousand having been sealed. Of the tribe of Naphtali, twelve thousand having been sealed. Of the tribe of Manasseh, twelve thousand having been sealed. 7. Of the tribe of Simeon, twelve thousand having been sealed. Of the tribe of Levi, twelve thousand having been sealed. Of the tribe of Issachar, twelve thousand having been sealed. 8. Of the tribe of Zebulun, twelve thousand having been sealed. Of the tribe of Joseph, twelve thousand having been sealed. Of the tribe of Benjamin, twelve thousand having been sealed. (Revelation 7:5-8)

The Jewish people will turn to Jesus, their Messiah when He returns. This preceding seven-year period will be exceptionally difficult for them. God's promise here is that He will be watching over them as a people through this time (Romans 11:25, 26).

For a long time, the Jews as a nation have not been considered the people of God because of their unfaithfulness (Hosea 1:6, 8, 9). The prophecy was that Israel would abide many days without a king, prince, sacrifice, and ephod (Hosea 3:4). There is grace individually for Jewish people who turn to the Lord Jesus Christ. In Christ, there is neither Jew nor Gentile but one church, His body (Colossians 3:11).

However, the purposes of God for the nation of Israel are that one day the people will turn to Him. He does not repent nor change His intentions (Romans 11:29-32). This national turning to Him will happen when Jesus returns. There will come a day when the nation recognises their Messiah. The recognition will cause Israel to mourn (Zechariah 12:10-14). Nationally they will be cleansed of their sin (Zechariah 13:1-3). This day of mourning and cleansing will be the fulfilment of the Day of Atonement they celebrate every year (Leviticus 23:27-32).

God before this will significantly chasten the nation. They will come to the point of utter ruin and destruction (Matthew 23:37-39). At the very moment when their murder is about to be finally accomplished the Lord Jesus shall return and rescue them (Zechariah 14:1-5). After the nation has returned to the Lord, there will be an annual feast of the harvest known as the Feast of Tabernacles which is a great feast of joy, which the whole earth will keep when Christ reigns on the planet for a thousand years (Zechariah 14:16). Again, the Jewish people celebrate this feast each year after the Day of Atonement. The prophetic act will see its fulfilment when Jesus returns (Leviticus 23:34-36).

Currently, Israel is no more godly or ungodly than any other nation. It is only those who have put their trust in Jesus the Messiah who are godly having the Holy Spirit. Many ungodly Jewish people are Jews by name alone and are not of the true Israel of God (Romans 2:28-29). The parable of the wheat and the tares applies to the nation of Israel also (Matthew 13:24-30, 37-43).

The 144,000 are the godly remnant of Israel who will remain faithful to the Lord in the seven-year period. They will refuse allegiance to false messiahs, and the antichrist. And God will keep them in this season. We see reference to faithful Jewish believers in the Prophet Daniel (Daniel 11:33-35, 12:1).

It was the practice among the Romans for soldiers to be marked on the hand, and for slaves to be branded in the forehead. According to Herodotus, in some instances the name of the god whom an individual worshipped people branded upon the worshipper. Similarly, the living God will publicly mark and acknowledged His own by branding their foreheads. The seal of the Holy Spirit indicates Divine ownership of Christians (Ephesians 1:13-14).

God's denotes ownership of His latter-day servants with His seal (Song of Solomon 8:6-7).

The Significance of One Hundred and Forty-Four Thousand

144=12x12=122

12 is a perfect number very much associated with government.

There were twelve Patriarchs from Seth to Noah and his family, and twelve from Shem to Jacob. There were thirteen attributed sons of Israel, Joseph's two sons, were included in the tribes, though actually, there are never more than twelve named in any one list. There are a number of listings, but in each record, one or the other is not included. Generally, it is Levi, but not always. In Revelation 7 both Dan and Ephraim are omitted, but the enumeration is still twelve, with Levi and Joseph listed for this special sealing.

There were also twelve Judges or Saviours. (See the book of Judges)

The Temple of Solomon has the number twelve as a predominating feature, in contrast with the Tabernacle, which has five. The Tabernacle emphasises grace, which is found symbolised in the tabernacle, and the government of the kingdom is in the Temple displayed by the number twelve.

Twelve legions of angels mark the perfection of angelic powers (Matthew 26:53).

The word palace in the New Testament occurs twelve times.

Dan and Ephraim were the first of Israel's tribes to go into idolatry (Judges 18:2, 20, 31). Could it be that the antichrist will be of the tribe of Dan (Genesis 49:17)? In the Millennial distribution of the land, God will restore both Dan and Ephraim, but Dan will be in the extreme north and farther away from the temple than any other of the tribes (Ezekiel 48). The pledge of security is not for these two rebellious tribes.

The meanings of the names are significant.

From this, we can learn a practical lesson on how to endure difficult times and circumstances. Seiss (Seiss, 1900, p. 168) translates them as follows:

Judah (confession or praise of God) The idea of praise, is to lift God up. The scene of the footballer being carried around on his teammate's shoulders at the end of a successful game and everyone celebrating the player is a secular example of praise. In times of trial and trouble, the safe place is to be always mindful of God's glory and reputation (1 Corinthians 10:31).

Reuben (viewing the Son) In difficulty, we need to keep out eyes on the Lord Jesus Christ (Hebrews 12:1-2).

Gad (a company) The encouragement of Christian fellowship, is also helpful in a time of difficulty (Malachi 3:16).

Asher (blessed) It is helpful to remember that those who are faithful to God, in a time of trial, are blessed by Him (James 1:12).

Naphtali (a wrestler or striving with) In times of trial and difficulty we are wrestling against the enemy. With God, we can overcome (Ephesians 6:10-12).

Manasseh (Forgetfulness) We are to forget the things of the world and fix our eyes upon heavenly treasure under challenging circumstances (Matthew 16:24-27).

Simeon (hearing and obeying) The only safe place in difficulty is to hear the Word of God and to obey the Lord (Jeremiah 7:23).

Levi (joined or cleaving to) Trouble should drive us to God and not from Him (Psalm 73:28).

Issachar (a reward or what is given by way of reward) There is a reward for those who are faithful in times of trouble (Hebrews 12:11).

Zebulun (a home or dwelling place) It is important to remember that God is our dwelling place in trouble (Psalm 46:1).

Joseph (added or an addition) God changes us in trouble and difficulty, and this is a good thing (James 1:2-4) even though trouble is not good.

Benjamin (son of the right hand, a son of old age) Testing is only for a season, and there will come a day when we are with the Lord where there will be no more trouble (Revelation 21:4).

2. The Gentiles

9. After these things I saw, and behold, a great crowd, who no one was able to number, out of all nations, and tribes, and people, and tongues, having stood before the throne and before the Lamb, having been clothed with white robes, and palm branches in their hands: 10. And crying with a great voice saying, Salvation to our God to the one sitting upon the throne, and to the Lamb. 11. And all the angels stood around the throne, and the elders and the four living beings, and fell before the throne upon their face, and they worshipped God, 12. Saying, Amen: Blessing, and glory, and wisdom, and thanksgiving, and honour, and power, and strength, to our God into the ages of the ages. Amen. (Revelation 7:9-12)

Here we see the 'fullness of the Gentiles' come in. There will also be a great company of non-Jewish people among the redeemed of the Lord. Undoubtedly during this tribulation time, many will be saved. It is not just harvest time for evil but also for righteousness. Both are coming to maturity (Matthew 13:37-42).

This company is not the church who are seen enthroned (Revelation 4:14). These stand before the throne.

The gospel will be proclaimed in at least three different ways. There will be many going around the world announcing the good news of salvation through Jesus Christ. Jesus himself emphasises this in His answer to the disciples about the end times (Matthew 24:14). There will be two very powerfully anointed witnesses in Jerusalem proclaiming the truth (Revelation 11:1-12). Thirdly in the heavens, there will be an angel heralding this (Revelation 14:6-7).

The Great Tribulation is a time unequalled for trouble and suffering (Matthew 24:21). These tribulation saints have: -

White robes (Revelation 7:9) This speaks of righteousness (Revelation 19:8).

Palms in their hands (Revelation 7:9). Palms speak of uprightness. The root meaning of the word palm is 'erect'. It gets its name from this quality. The righteous are flourishing as a palm (Psalms 92:12).

13. And one of the elders answered, saying to me, These having been clothed with white robes, who are they and from where did they come? 14. And I said to him, Lord, you know. And he said to me, These are the ones coming out of the great trouble, and they washed their robes and whitened them in the blood of the Lamb. 15. Because of this, they are before the throne of God, and they serve him day and night in his inner shrine of the temple: And the one sitting upon the throne will pitch a tent upon them. 16. They will not hunger again, nor thirst anymore: neither will fall upon them the sun, nor any heat. 17. Because the Lamb in the middle of the throne will shepherd them, and he will lead them upon springs of living water: and God will wipe out every teardrop from their eyes. (Revelation 7:13-17)

The elder is distinct from this company. As we saw in Revelation 4 and 5, the elders speak of the church and those redeemed from the earth caught up during the Rapture. This company of Gentile, non-Jewish believers have been saved during the Tribulation. They stand in heaven indicating they were martyred during this time. Not every believer will be martyred during the Tribulation. It is clear that when Jesus judges the living nations at His return, a group of godly people will be rewarded (Matthew 25:33-40). This martyred group in heaven will be resurrected when Jesus comes to the earth (Revelation 20:4).

Those who are saved during the Tribulation will be saved on the same basis as all those who have gone before. There is only one Gospel (Galatians 1:6-10). Salvation is obtained through faith in the Lord Jesus Christ. There is no other way (John 14:6), and there is no other name whereby people are saved (Acts 4:12).

The hope that every true believer has is incredible. We are told there will be no more hunger, thirst, no more tears and that we will live with God forever with no more threat or pain. It is this hope which enables believers to endure in great tribulation. When we are facing difficulties in our lives, we can encourage ourselves by remembering the hope we have. We need to learn to encourage ourselves in the Lord as David did when he faced very challenging circumstances (1 Samuel 30:6).

Revelation 8

1. And when he opened the seventh seal, there was silence in heaven for about half an hour. 2. And I saw seven angels who stood before God: and there was given to them seven trumpets. 3. And another angel came, and stood at the altar, having a golden censer: and there was given to him much incense, which he might offer with the prayers of all the saints upon the golden altar before the throne. 4. And the smoke of the incenses, ascended with the prayers of the saints, out of the hand of the angel before God. 5. And the angel had taken the censer, he filled it out of the fire of the altar, and he threw it into the earth: and voices, thunders, lightnings and an earthquake happened. (Revelation 8:1-5)

The Seventh Seal

Three things happen when Jesus breaks the seventh seal. There is silence in heaven for about half an hour, seven angels appear with seven trumpets, and another angel offers incense with the prayers of God's people.

The Silence of Heaven

For heaven to be silenced what is taking place must be genuinely momentous. Subjection to authority is symbolised by silence (I Timothy 2:11). Heaven is learning from God in submission. In what God is doing in judgment, He will also put to silence the ignorance of foolish men, though admittedly they are not in Heaven (1 Peter 2:15).

The Trumpets

We see trumpets used for war, for a gathering, for travelling and days of gladness, (Numbers 10:1-10). In the same way, these seven trumpets herald:

- War (Revelation 19:11)

- Assembling (1 Thessalonians 4:16-18)

- Journeys End (Hebrews 12:1-2)

- Days of Gladness (Jude 1:24)

The seven trumpets appear in consequence of breaking the last seal. They are part of this process. All three sets of judgments, seals, trumpets, and bowls, conclude with the return of the Lord since they have the same endpoint. It is after the breaking of the seventh seal that every creature in heaven, on earth and under the earth acknowledge that Jesus is Lord, (Revelation 5:13). After the seventh trumpet, the kingdoms of the world are in submission to the Lord, (Revelation 11:15). Understanding the placing the trumpet judgments within the breaking of the seventh seal is essential for a correct understanding of the chronology of events within the Tribulation.

Incense and Prayer

Incense is symbolic of prayer (Psalm 141:2). When we pray, there are others who pray with us adding their fragrance to our prayers which is why we can be confident God hears our prayers. The Holy Spirit adds His incense (Romans 8:26). Jesus adds His perfume to our prayers (Hebrews 7:25). When Israel fought against Amalek, there was a remarkable picture of prayer with the support of two others. Aaron and Hur helped Moses to hold up the rod of God in his hands until Israel won the battle against Amalek (Exodus 17:8-13). The High Priest Aaron pictures our Great High Priest Jesus supporting us in our prayers and Hur pictures the Holy Spirit. We can, therefore, be confident that we have the rod of God (power) in our hands when we pray and that the Father will indeed answer our prayers. Once again, we see the Trinity functioning together (James 5:16-18).

Under the law, the High Priest used a golden censer to carry fire from the brazen altar to the golden altar of incense (Leviticus 16:12). The eighth angel, therefore, assumed the character of the High Priest. The High Priest had access to the golden altar in the earthly tabernacle, so the angel occupied the place of High Priest in the heavenly sphere. The reference, therefore, is to the Lord Jesus Christ, the Great High Priest. The angel here is none other than the Lord Jesus Christ.

The incense (Exodus 30:34-35) offered up by the High Priest consisted of:

Stacte - It means to fall in drops, figuratively to prophesy. The prayers of the Lord Jesus are the very Words of God (John 1:1).

Onycha - The root meaning of the word is to roar like a lion. The Lord will roar like a lion in the last days (Jeremiah 25:30).

Galbanum - The root meaning is the richest or choicest part. The prayers of Jesus are the most select part of the supplication made to the Father (Matthew 3:17).

Frankincense - This takes its name from its whiteness. There is such purity in the Lord Jesus our intercessor (Psalm 12:6).

Salted - This is what the phrase tempered together means. Salt is a great purifier and also adds taste to what is bland. These were two uses of salt in the ancient world. There is a purifying effect upon our prayers through the intercession of the Lord Jesus. He makes our prayers palatable to God, the Father (Ezekiel 43:24).

There are times when Jesus is described as an angel. And to further complicate things angels are also sometimes described as men. For example:

The man that Jacob wrestled with was Jesus. The man wrestling with Jacob said, "Why do you ask me my name?" He would not reveal His name at that point since the time for the name of Jesus to be revealed had not yet come. Jacob says that he saw God face to face (Genesis 32:24-30).

The man who stood before Joshua was Jesus. Angels never permit themselves to be worshipped, and yet Joshua worshipped at this point (Joshua 5:13-15).

Manoah and his wife met Jesus. He would not tell them His name since it was wonderful (Judges 13:17-22).

There is at least one other occasion in Revelation when the Lord Jesus is described as an angel. Remember the word angel means a messenger and it can apply to men or spirits or any being fulfilling that role. The fact that here Jesus is described as the eighth angel is significant. The numerical equivalent of His name, Jesus, is 888. The ancient world counted with their alphabets, and as such, any word in the Bible has an equivalent number. Contrast this with the number of the beast, which is 666.

The prayers of the saints are connected with the sounding of the trumpets. God is moving in response to the cry of His people and remembering them even when judgment is taking place.

The Seven Trumpets

The seven seals divide into four and three with the first four seals being horses and the last three being distinct from these. The seven trumpets also split into four and three with the final three horns described as woes.

First Trumpet, Hail Mingled with Blood

6. And the seven angels the ones having the seven trumpets prepared themselves that they might sound the trumpets. 7. And the first angel sounded the trumpet, and there happened hailstone and fire having been mingled with blood, and it was thrown into the earth: and the third of trees was burnt up, and all the green grass was burnt up. (Revelation 8:6, 7)

In the seven seals, trumpets and bowls we see repeated links to the plagues of Egypt. The Egyptian plagues foretold the judgement upon this earth and its gods. The first trumpet corresponds to the seventh Egyptian plague of hail (Exodus 9:22-25). Since the Egypt plague was literal, there is a good reason for assuming there will be a literal fulfilment of this plague upon the earth. The result of this will be a third of the earth and trees destroyed and all the grass.

Trying to imagine this plague from a literal point of view, the preceding worldwide earthquake in the sixth seal would have caused severe weather phenomena. Severe hail could well be within this. Given the shifting of the earth's crust about the mantle of the planet, there will be severe volcanic activity. Volcanic material would undoubtedly be released into the atmosphere of the planet falling with the hail. Hence the hail mingled with fire. The effect upon trees and green grass would be devastating.

However, as with any miraculous move of God, there is always an element of this being a sign of a spiritual truth. The trees and the grass are the targets of this hail. Trees speak of kings (Daniel 4:20-22). Trees are a type of mankind (Judges 9:8-15). Grass speaks of mortal men (I Peter 1:24).

From this, we see two things, at the literal level we see a third of the trees and grass consumed which would have a significant impact on those living on the earth at this time. More figuratively we note that this plague is pictured as destroying a third of mankind and their rulers during this period.

Second Trumpet, The Great Mountain Burning

8. And the second angel sounded the trumpet, and as it were a great mountain burning with fire was thrown into the sea: and the third of the sea became blood: 9. And the third part of the creatures in the sea, the ones having life, died, and the third of the ships were destroyed.
(Revelation 8:8, 9)

The first judgement on Egypt involved water becoming blood (Exodus 7:14-24). Thus, we see a correspondence with the second trumpet. Literally, we see a third of the earth's seas and oceans affected with a third of life in the sea dying including ships and their passengers. Perhaps an asteroid colliding with the sea could bring such a catastrophe. An exploding volcano could also create a situation where a burning mountain falls into the sea. The word for sea here is in the singular. It is hard therefore to judge if more than one sea is affected. When Biblically the sea is mentioned without being named it often refers to the Mediterranean. In Hebrew 'the great sea' is a proper noun and means invariably the Mediterranean Sea (Lang, 1973, pp. 78-80). The impact would be of a different order of magnitude if a third of the inhabitants of the Mediterranean Sea were destroyed as opposed to a more world-wide disaster.

Figuratively mountains speak of kingdoms or established powers in scripture (Daniel 2:44, 45). God's judgement upon Babylon is described as a burning mountain (Jeremiah 51:25). The sea is a picture of the wicked people of the earth (Isaiah 57:20). Thus, we see God's judgement upon a kingdom which results in a third of mankind destroyed.

Third Trumpet, Wormwood

10. And the third angel sounded the trumpet, and a great star burning as a lamp, fell out of the heaven, and it fell upon a third of the rivers, and upon the springs of waters: 11. And the name of the star is said to be, Wormwood: and the third part of the waters became wormwood: and many men died of the waters because they were made bitter. (Revelation 8:10, 11)

A literal fulfilment of this could occur when a meteor composed of a frozen liquid mass struck the earth. This meteor strike could well have a polluting quality upon the drinking waters of the earth. There would be a poisoning of fresh water sources, given the drinking water a bitter taste and many dying.

Stars are representative of heavenly powers (Job 38:7). This great star cast into the sea speaks of a heavenly power thrown down upon the earth. We see Satan and his angels grounded upon the earth at this time (Revelation 12:7-9) which results in a corruption of the waters. The waters we have seen are evil men. The star is called Wormwood which means bitter. We get the drink Absinth from this term because of its bitter taste. It will not be good news for mankind that the Devil is grounded (Revelation 12:12).

Fourth Trumpet, Partial Darkness

12. And the fourth angel sounded the trumpet, and the third part of the sun was struck, the third part of the moon and the third part of the stars: so that the third part of them might be darkened, the third part of the day cannot shine, and the night likewise. (Revelation 8:12)

The ninth plague upon Egypt was darkness (Exodus 10:21-23). There may well be a literal darkness at this time upon the earth. The third part of them being darkened could refer to a dimming of the sun by a third regarding its brightness at this point. Given the extreme volcanic and earthquake activity preceding this plague, a vast amount of material may have been ejected into the earth's atmosphere. This material could well reduce light levels from the sun, moon and stars.

There will undoubtedly be a spiritual darkness upon many (Matthew 24:24). Mankind becomes more and more darkened as the iniquity of humanity comes to full maturity (2 Timothy 3:1-8). Note the reference in (2 Timothy) to the judgements in Exodus with Jannes and Jambres resisting Moses. Similarly, there will be men energised by Satan who will oppose the truth. Two are known as the Beast from the Sea, and the other is called the Beast from the Land (Revelation 13).

Evil has a life cycle from conception to full growth. When full growth comes, judgement falls (James 1:15). In Abraham's day, the iniquity of the people of Canaan had not come to full growth. The judgement did not fall until hundreds of years later (Genesis 15:12-16). Some individuals sin and their sin reaches maturity. At this point, people commit a final sin that triggers judgement. This iniquity is known as a sin unto death (1 John 5:16-17). Judgement always falls at this point. Ananias and Sapphira was an example of this (Acts 5:1-11). Please note this even happens in the days of grace we now enjoy. Sodom and Gomorrah as a city sinned unto death in the way the city treated the angels when they stayed at Lot's house (Genesis 19:4-11).

An Angel Flying in the Midst of Heaven

The chapter closes with an angel announcing the last three trumpets naming then as woes.

13. And I saw and heard one angel flying in mid-heaven saying with a great voice, Woe, woe, woe to the ones dwelling on the earth, of the remaining sounds of the trumpet of the three angels, who are about to blow the trumpet. (Revelation 8:13)

Depending on the Greek text the Bible version has been translated from, the word angel is replaced by the word eagle. The Majority Text and the Westcott-Hort Text have an eagle. The Textus Receptus has an angel. The eagle moves swiftly against its prey. So, God's judgement is no longer delayed but coming quickly (Job 9:26) and (Habakkuk 1:8). Contextually an angel is more likely since he is speaking. Eagles don't speak, but angels do

Revelation 9

1. And the fifth angel blew the trumpet, and I saw a star having fallen out of the heaven to the earth: and the key of the pit of the abyss was given to him. 2. And he opened the pit of the abyss: and smoke ascended out of the pit, as smoke of a great furnace: and the sun was darkened and the air by the smoke of the pit. 3. And out of the smoke came a locust swarm into the earth: and power was given to them as the scorpions of the earth have power. 4. And it was said to them that they might not harm the grass of the earth, nor any greenery, nor any tree: except the men everyone who have not the seal of God upon their foreheads. 5. And it was given to them that they might not kill them, but that they might torture five months: and their torture is as the torture of a scorpion when it strikes a man. 6. And in those days men will seek death, and they will not find it: and they will desire to die, and death will flee from them. 7. And the appearances of the locust swarm like horses having been prepared to war: and upon their heads as victors' crowns like to gold, and their faces as faces of men. 8. And they were having hair as the hair of women, and their teeth were as lions. 9. And they were having breastplates, as breastplates made of iron: and the sound of their wings as a sound of chariots of many horses running into battle. 10. And they have tails like scorpions, and stings were in their tails: And their power to harm men five months. 11. And they have over them a king, the angel of the abyss: The name for him in Hebrew, Abaddon, and in the Greek, he has the name, Apollyon. 12. The one woe has departed: Behold, there come still two woes after these things. (Revelation 9:1-11)

Fifth Trumpet - First Woe, Locusts

The source of this first woe is from the Bottomless Pit, often translated Abyss in modern versions of the Bible. The term bottomless pit is mentioned seven times in Revelation. These are (Revelation 9:1, 2, 11; 11:7; 17:8; 20:1, 3). The word 'bottomless pit' is sometimes translated 'deep.' It is a place where spirits are imprisoned (Jude 1:6). The legion of demons in the Gadarene man pleaded with Jesus not to be sent into the deep, i.e. the abyss (Luke 8:31). Jesus went to this place when He died and preached to the spirits there (1 Peter 3:19), (Romans 10:6-7). Also, we know Jesus went to Paradise with the dying thief who turned to Him (Luke 23:43). In the blowing of the fifth trumpet at least some of these imprisoned spirits are released into the earth. The abyss would seem to be within the planet and would appear to be therefore another section of hell specifically for fallen angels and demons.

Locusts

These are tormenting spirits and are likened to locusts. The eighth plague of Egypt was the plague of locusts (Exodus 10:12-20). They were also compared unto scorpions. Scorpions and chastisement are linked together in scripture (1 Kings 12:11). So, we see these evil spirits being used to punish men. The scorpion tail is a reference to Satan (Luke 10:18, 19). In those days, there will be many who will be in torment, which is spiritual in its origin and is the ultimate fulfilment of the locusts referred to in (Joel 1:2-7).

They only had power over those who had not the seal of God on their foreheads. People who give themselves to evil; open the door to fallen spirits. King Saul was an example of this (1 Samuel 16:14). Every true Christian has been sealed with the Holy Spirit (Ephesians 1:13). Therefore, we need never fear tormenting spirits.

They are:

Horses prepared unto battle. Horses link to warfare in scripture (Jeremiah 46:3-4). These spirits are warring against men (Joel 2:7). We see in the description of Joel 2 a very similar report of the locusts in Revelation 9.

On their heads having crowns of gold. The word for diadem is the victor's crown. They will overcome the men they war against (2 Peter 2:19).

Their hair was the hair of women. Hair speaks of glory (1 Corinthians 11:15). Depending on the context it can be a vainglory and pride. Absalom took great pride in his hair (2 Samuel 14:26). It resulted in Absalom's downfall (2 Samuel 18:9). The vainglory linked to these spirits will be their downfall.

They had the teeth of lions. The teeth of lions devour (Psalm 57:4). Locusts devour vegetation, but these eat men without killing them (1 Peter 5:8).

They had breastplates of iron. Iron is sturdy, breaks into pieces and subdues all things (Daniel 2:41). We see these spirits being too powerful for wicked men, conquering and cutting them into pieces.

Their wings sounded like horses and chariots in battle. Chariots were the tanks of the ancient world and were devastating in combat. They also speak of trusting in natural strength (Psalm 20:7).

They could hurt men five months. Five is the number of grace. It is only the kindness of God that the torment is of limited duration. Thankfully the principalities and powers have limitations set by God on them that they cannot exceed. God limited the suffering of Job coming from Satan (Job 2:6).

Their king is Abaddon (Apollyon). Both names mean destroying angel. Satan is a killer and a destroyer (John 10:10), (John 8:44).

Sixth Trumpet - Second Woe, Angels Linked to the Euphrates

13. And the sixth angel blew the trumpet, and I heard one voice from the four horns of the golden altar before God, 14. Saying to the sixth angel who was having the trumpet, Loose the four angels the ones having been bound upon the great river Euphrates. 15. And they loosed the four angels the ones having been prepared into the hour, and day, and month, and year, that they might kill the third of men. 16. And the number of military campaigners' cavalry horses were two myriads of myriads: and I heard their number. 17. And in this way I saw the horses in the vision, and the ones sitting upon them having breastplates fiery-red and hyacinth (blue) and sulphurous (yellow): and the heads of the horses as heads of lions: and out of their mouths comes out fire, and smoke, and sulphur. 18. By these three were killed the third of men, by the fire, and by the smoke, and by the sulphur, coming out of their mouths. 19. For their power is in their mouth, and in their tails: for their tails are like snakes, having heads, and with them, they harm. (Revelation 9:13-19)

Four angels were loosed prepared for an hour, and a day, and a month. Everything that happens only happens in God's perfect timing. Evil is held back until the right time (2 Peter 3:8-9). Our lives are in God's perfect timing (Psalm 31:15).

The number of the horsemen were 200 million which is a vast army - a world judgement indeed. Twenty is the number of expectancy. Twenty years Jacob waited to get possession of his wives and property (Genesis 31:38, 41). Two hundred seems connected with insufficiency (John 6:7). Twenty and two hundred have been multiplied here by factors of ten million and one million respectively. Figuratively we have an incredible expectancy of mankind getting their just deserts before God and their insufficiency to stand on that day. Commentators are divided here as to the question of these horsemen. Are they spirits that are allowed to kill men or are they actual people being motivated by these four angels that were bound at the Euphrates? The fact that we are told that they kill men by what comes out of their mouths would indicate they are not men but a Satanic army. Unlike the previous trumpet men were tormented by spirits here, they are killed.

Their breastplates were fire, jacinth and brimstone. The first mention of fire and brimstone in the Bible is the raining down of fire and brimstone (sulphur) on Sodom and Gomorrah (Genesis 19:24). The last mention is the Lake of Fire (Revelation 21:8). This vast army is the agent of God's wrath. Jacinth gets its name from the deep blue colour. Blue is associated with the keeping of the law (Numbers 15:37-41). The nations of the world have failed to keep the law and as such are paying the penalty of this.

Their power was in their mouth and tails. Although there is a physical conflict spoken of here, it is rooted in the teaching of lies. Isaiah says that the teacher of lies is the tail (Isaiah 9:15). The mouth and the tail link to false prophets. As we shall see in Revelation 16 unclean spirits come out of the mouths of the dragon, beast and false prophet (Revelation 16:13).

20. And the rest of men, the ones not killed in these plagues, neither they repented from the works of their hands, that they might not worship demons, and idols of gold, and silver, and bronze, and stone, and wood: which neither are able to see, nor to hear, nor to walk about. 21. And they repented not of their murders, nor from their sorceries, nor from their sexual immoralities, nor from their thefts. (Revelation 9:20, 21)

Despite all these judgements men repented not. Judgement never brings men unto repentance. The mercy of God brings men unto repentance, (Romans 2:4). One of the most amazing features of the Tribulation is the mercy of God in presenting the truth to people again and again. Those who hear the truth and repeatedly reject it become hardened. Eventually, they become unreachable and are described as vessels of anger prepared to destruction (Romans 9:22). As the time for Jesus to stand upon the earth comes nearer so unrepentant men become wickeder and wickeder (2 Timothy 3:1-9). We are told that those who are often corrected by God but don't change are suddenly destroyed (Proverbs 29:1). Let us, therefore, be quick to change when God corrects us.

Revelation 10

Another Parenthesis

There was a gap in the account of the seven seals with an insertion between the sixth and seventh seal. Similarly, there is a gap between the sixth trumpet and the seventh. Later we will also see that there is a gap between the sixth and seventh bowl of wrath (Revelation 16:13-15). This parenthesis divides into three sections.

1. And I saw another strong angel coming down out of the heaven, having been clothed with a cloud: and a rainbow upon the head, and his face as the sun, and his feet as pillars of fire: 2. And he was having in his hand a little book having been opened: and his right foot he put upon the sea, but the left upon the earth. 3. And he cried with a great voice, just as a lion roars: and when he cried, the seven thunders spoke their voices. 4. And when the seven thunders had spoken their voices, I was about to write: and I heard a voice out of the heaven, saying to me, Seal what the seven thunders said, and do not write these things. 5. And the angel I saw having stood upon the sea and upon the earth raised his hand to the heaven, 6. And he swore by the one living into the ages of the ages, who created the heaven, and the things in it, and the earth, and the things in it, and the sea, and the things in it, that time will not be again: 7. But in the days of the sound of the seventh angel, when he is about to blow the trumpet, and the mystery of God will finish, as he proclaimed to his servants the prophets. (Revelation 10:1-7)

The Mighty Angel

The Mighty Angel is none other than the Lord Jesus Christ. We also saw Him described as an angel in (Revelation 8:3-5) which is evident because of the following reasons: -

He is mighty (Revelation 10:1). The word means strong. The Lord is strong and mighty (Psalm 24:8).

He is clothed with a cloud (Revelation 10:1). The Lord went in a pillar of cloud before Israel (Exodus 13:21). The glory of God manifests in a cloud (Exodus 16:10; 24:16). The Holiest of Holies had the cloud hovering over the Ark of the Covenant (Leviticus 16:2). The Temple of Solomon also had the cloud of Glory (1 Kings 8:10, 11). The cloud of glory departed from the Temple in Ezekiel's day (Ezekiel 10:4, 18). In the Transfiguration, the cloud was linked with the Lord Jesus (Matthew 17:5). When Jesus ascended, a cloud received Him out of the disciples' sight (Acts 1:9). When Jesus returns, He will be within a cloud (Luke 21:27).

A rainbow is upon His head (Revelation 10:1). The rainbow connects with the only other reference to the word 'rainbow' in the New Testament, which is surrounding the throne of God (Revelation 4:3). We saw the rainbow joined to God keeping covenant with the Earth even in judgement.

His face was like the sun (Revelation 10:1). Jesus is so described in other parts of the Bible (Revelation 1:16).

His feet were like pillars of fire (Revelation 10:1). Again, this is the description of the Lord Jesus at the start of Revelation (Revelation 1:15).

A little book was open in His hand, (Revelation 10:2). We saw the sealed scroll being taken by the Lord Jesus and the seals being opened previously in Revelation. At this point, he is about to return, and thus the book is open, the seal judgements having happened (Revelation 5:7). It seems unlikely that this is the same book as the mighty scroll of the title deeds of the earth. The word used is a diminutive of the word for the scroll used in Revelation 5. A smaller portion of this inheritance is in His hand specifically to be given to John. All we possess we receive through Jesus. He takes of what he has been given and gives a portion to us.

His right foot was on the sea and His left foot on the land (Revelation 10:2). All things are beneath the feet of Jesus. In other words, He rules over all (Hebrews 2:8).

He cried as a lion roars (Revelation 10:3). We have already seen the Lord Jesus described as the lion in Revelation (Revelation 5:5).

Seven Thunders Respond (Revelation 10:3). When Jesus cried out to the Father upon earth, the Father responded, and the people around thought it was thundering (John 12:27-29). John was not allowed to write what the seven thunders uttered. Not everything that God reveals to a prophet is to be spoken (2 Corinthians 12:3, 4).

He lifted His hand up to heaven (Revelation 10:5). Another example of this is at the end of the book of Daniel (Daniel 12:7). Looking at the description of this man, it would appear He is the Lord Jesus Christ appearing to Daniel (Daniel 10:5, 6). In both Daniel and Revelation, the prophet had to be picked up off the ground having encountered this person. Compare (Daniel 10:10, 11) with (Revelation 1:17). The Lord Jesus is ever living to make intercession with lifted up hands (1 Timothy 2:8) and (Hebrews 7:25).

He swears by God (Revelation 10:6). God swears by Himself (Hebrews 6:13-18).

Time no longer (Revelation 10:6) In Greek, there are different words for time meaning slightly different things. Here the word means a space of time, which by implication means delay. Thus, the Lord is saying there will be no more delay. God has delayed so that men might turn to Him and repent (2 Peter 3:9). There always comes the point when this space to repent ends which was the case in the days of Noah when the flood came. The 120 years were given for men to repent (Genesis 6:3). Those who do not repent become hardened and their evil comes to full maturity. At that point judgement falls (Ecclesiastes 8:11-13).

The mystery of God will be finished (Revelation 10:7). The mystery has been declared by the prophets. In other words, every promise and purpose of God, which He has declared, will be fulfilled. All the stuff we don't understand will be made clear. A mystery is something hidden which will be made known at its proper time, for example (Colossians 1:26).

Eating the Book

8. And the voice which I heard out of heaven, again speaking with me and saying, Go, take the little book the one having been opened in the hand of the angel the one having stood upon the sea and upon the earth. 9. And I came to the angel saying to him, Give me the little book. And he says to me, Take and devour it: and it will make your stomach bitter, but in your mouth, it will be sweet as honey. 10. And I took the little book out of the hand of the angel, and I devoured it: and it was sweet in my mouth as sweet honey: and when I ate it, it made my stomach bitter. 11. And he says to me, It is necessary for you to prophesy again over peoples, and nations, and tongues, and many kings. (Revelation 10:8-11)

The commissioning of a prophet is pictured as the eating of a book (Ezekiel 2:7–10). John is receiving a message that he might prophesy again. The second half of Revelation (Revelation 12-22) is this message. The sweetness in the mouth but the bitterness in the belly is that the prophet delights to receive the word from God, but the message in both Ezekiel's and John case was a message of judgement. The eating in the mouth and then going into the belly is a picture of meditation which is the process of assimilating the Word of God and making it part of who we are. Chewing the cud is a picture of meditation also (Leviticus 11:1-8). Becoming doers of the Word of God is accomplished by meditation (James 1:22). This process is known as sanctification (1 Thessalonians 4:3-4). The initial hearing of the Word of God is sweet (Psalm 19:10, 119:103). The process of becoming a doer can be bitter (Proverbs 20:30).

Revelation 11

1. And there was given to me a reed like a stick: and the angel had stood, saying, To rise, and measure the inner shrine of God, and the altar, and the ones worshipping in it. 2. And the courtyard, the outside of the inner shrine leave out and measure it not: because it has been given to the nations: and the holy city they will trample forty-two months. 3. And I will give power to my two witnesses, and they will prophesy one thousand two hundred and sixty days, having been clothed in sackcloth. 4. These are the two olive trees, and the two lampstands which have taken their stand before the God of the earth. 5. And if someone may wish to harm them, fire comes out of their mouths and devours their enemies: and if someone may wish to harm them, in this way it is necessary for him to be killed. 6. These have authority to close the heaven that it might not drench rain in the days of their prophecy: and they have authority over the waters, to turn them into blood, and to strike the earth with every plague, whenever they may wish. 7. And when they finish their witness, the wild animal the one rising up out of the abyss will make war with them, and he will conquer them and will kill them, 8. And their corpses will be upon the street of the great city, which is called spiritually Sodom and Egypt, where also our Lord was crucified. 9. And they out of the peoples, and tribes, and tongues, and nations will see the corpses three and a half days, and they will not permit their corpses to be put into tombs. 10. And the ones dwelling upon the earth will rejoice over them, and make merry, and send gifts to one another: because these two prophets tormented the ones dwelling upon the earth. 11. And after the three and a half days, the Spirit of life from God entered into them, and they stood upon their feet: and great fear fell upon the ones seeing them. 12. And they heard a great voice from the heaven saying to them, Come up here. And they ascended into heaven in the cloud: and their enemies saw them. 13. And in that hour a great earthquake happened, and a tenth of the city fell, and seven thousand named men were killed in the earthquake: and the rest became afraid and gave glory to the God of the heaven. 14. The second woe departed: and behold, the third woe comes quickly. (Revelation 11:1-14)

The Gospel Proclaimed by the Two Witnesses

Measuring the Temple (Revelation 11:1) Measuring in scripture marks off what is God's, (Zechariah 2:1-5). Measuring also denotes what comes under God's judgement (Isaiah 65:7).

The Gentiles treading the city underfoot (Revelation 11:2) Forty-two months is three and a half years which is also 1260 days. We know that halfway through the seven-year period, that so much of Revelation focuses on; there will be significant events. A treaty will fracture that will result in considerable persecution for the people of God and the Jewish nation (Daniel 9:27). As we have previously seen the week, spoken of as a 'seven', is a seven-year period. At this time, there will be a temple in Jerusalem, which shall be violated. Jerusalem will itself be downtrodden for three and a half years (Mark 13:14-19).

The Two Witnesses (Revelation 11:3-14) During this challenging time God will have faithful witnesses for Himself. They will witness in both the power of Elijah who stopped the rain for three and a half years and in the ability of Moses to turn water into blood. They are spoken of in (Zechariah 4:1-5; 11-14). There is a need for two in order to establish their testimony, (Deuteronomy 17:6). It would seem that the two witnesses are teaching the truth during the first half of the Tribulation. There will be some religious freedom still up to the breaking of the seven-year treaty. With the breaking of the treaty and the destruction of world religions will come the absolute necessity to worship the Beast from the Sea. Thus, the two witnesses will be martyred at this midpoint after their testimony is complete. Since the followers of Jesus were told to flee Jerusalem when the treaty is broken, it would seem unthinkable that the two witnesses would remain in Jerusalem in direct contradiction to what Jesus said. This is another indication that they witnessed in the first half of the Tribulation.

Fire devours their enemies (Revelation 11:5). Elijah had the power to call fire down upon his enemies (2 Kings 1:9-15). The judgement of hail mingled with fire may well be as a result of these prophets calling down fire upon the ungodly.

They have the power to stop it raining (Revelation 11:6). In other words, these witnesses will be moving in the spirit and energy of Elijah (1 Kings 17:1) which is the ultimate fulfilment of the prophecy that Elijah would come (Malachi 4:5). Interestingly the witness of Elijah in Ahab's time pointed to the witness in the last days. Note the time it did not rain was for three and a half years (James 5:17, 18). It would seem that during the first half of the Tribulation there will be an extended time of drought.

They have the power to turn water into blood. (Revelation 11:6) Again we see the two witnesses functioning in the power of Moses (Exodus 4:9). The Transfiguration is a remarkable picture of the Lord Jesus returning in glory. Note in the light of the two witnesses it is appropriate that both Elijah and Moses appear at the Transfiguration, (Matthew 17:1-3). It may well be the waters being turned into blood in the second trumpet judgement was called down and prophesied by these two witnesses.

The city where Jesus was crucified (Revelation 11:8) This detail, therefore, identifies it as Jerusalem. Here it is also likened unto Sodom and Egypt. Sodom was evil (Genesis 13:13). Thus, fire was appropriate for its judgement (Genesis 19:24). Egypt displayed great violence against the people of God (Exodus 1:8-16; 22). It was wholly appropriate that the Egyptians should drink the blood they shed from the place they the babies died. So, will violent men drink of the blood they have poured out in that day (Revelation 16:4-7). God has, from the flood, said that those who shed blood would have their blood spilt by men. This is what the drinking of waters turned to blood symbolises (Genesis 9-6). Literally, of course, the waters may well be blood red in colour.

The Seventh Trumpet, The Third Woe, Jesus Reigns

The seventh trumpet speaks of the return of the Lord with the kingdoms of the world becoming His, (Philippians 2:10, 11). It is important to realise that this trumpet is sounded for many days (Revelation 10:7). The sounding of this trumpet may well be from the midpoint of the Tribulation unto its end. While this trumpet is sounding the last seven judgements of the bowls will be poured out.

15. And the seventh angel blew the trumpet: and there came great voices in the heaven, saying, The kingdoms of the world became of our Lord, and of his Christ: and he will reign into the ages of the ages. 16. And the twenty-four elders the ones sitting before God upon their thrones, fell on their faces and worshipped God. 17. Saying, We give thanks to you, O Lord the Almighty God, the one being and the one who was and the one coming: because you have taken your great power, and you have reigned. 18. And the nations were angry, and your anger came, and the time of the dead to be judged, and to give the wages to your servants, to the prophets, and to the saints, and the ones fearing your name, to the small and the great: and to destroy the ones destroying the earth. 19. And the inner shrine of the temple of God was opened in the heaven, and the ark of his covenant was seen in his inner shrine: And lightnings, and voices, and thunders, and an earthquake, and great hail happened. (Revelation 11:15-19)

The One who is and who was and who is to come (Revelation 11:17). The name Jehovah is a compound of three Hebrew words, 'He will be,' 'Being,' and 'He was.' The name Jesus comes from the Hebrew for Joshua which means Jehovah is Salvation. Thus, in both the name of the Father and the Son we see their eternal nature. In the same way, we note their rule is forever.

And the nations were angry (Revelation 11:18) Fallen man has severe anger against God. Their fury and unity is against the Father, Son and Holy Spirit and was foretold in the Psalms with the outcome of the return of Jesus defeating and judging the nations (Psalm 2).

And the time of the dead that they should be judged, (Revelation 11:18) In the seventh trumpet we see that the Lord Jesus returns. After Jesus returns, there is a thousand-year reign of Christ upon earth, ending with a final rebellion and fire coming down and destroying those who rebel at the end of the Millennium. The final resurrection of the wicked for eternal judgement follows the Millennium (Revelation 20:7-15).

The Ark of His testament will appear (Revelation 11:19) Whenever sinful man looked upon the Ark uncovered judgement fell upon them. The men of Bethshemesh saw the Ark and judgement fell upon them (1 Samuel 6:19). Uzzah was slain for touching the Ark (2 Samuel 6:6-7). The Ark was covered by the tabernacle, which was a cloth (Exodus 26:1). When the Ark was being carried it was also covered with a series of cloths (Numbers 4:5, 6). These coverings teach of the Lord Jesus. He is the one who has covered, thus saving those who believe in Him from the judgement of God. The word atonement means covering (Leviticus 1:4). The wicked will not be able to avail themselves of the covering of the Lord Jesus when God manifests in judgement. The Ark of the Covenant is a remarkable picture of God. Just as the Ark consisted of a box with the law written in it and a lid called the mercy seat, so in God mercy and Truth are met together (Psalm 85:10).

Revelation 12

Seven Characters

In chapters 12 to 14, some of the leading figures within the end time events appear.

The Woman

1. And a great sign was seen in the heaven: a woman having been clothed with the sun, and the moon beneath her feet, and upon her head a victor's crown of twelve stars: (Revelation 12:1)

The woman is a picture of the nation of Israel. The sun, moon and twelve stars figuratively were used to describe Joseph's family in one of his dreams (Genesis 37:9-10). Israel prophetically is spoken of as a woman giving birth to a child (Jeremiah 4:31). The child is Jesus, the Messiah (Micah 5:2, 3). The fact that she has been given two wings like an eagle indicates fast flight as in escape (Deuteronomy 28:49). Jesus talks about the time when Israel will have to flee into the wilderness (Matthew 24:16). Some people think they will escape to the ancient city of Petra because of a prophecy in (Isaiah 16:1-4). Compare this with (Psalm 60:9). The time of this sanctuary in the desert will be three and a half years. i.e. 1260 days (Revelation 12:6) or a 'time, times and half a time' (Revelation 12:14).

The Child

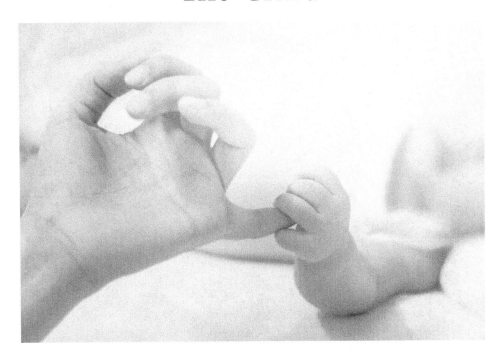

2. And in the womb having a child she cries, suffering birth-pangs, and being pained to bear a child. (Revelation 12:2)

As we have already seen the child is Jesus. Remember Revelation often looks at the future, sometimes at the present and also looks at past events (Revelation 1:19).

There was an ongoing attack from Satan to prevent the Messiah from ever being born. Satan made a determined effort to destroy Jesus during His time on earth. Much suffering has come to the nation of Israel as a consequence of this. God declared His intention to send Jesus from the fall in the Garden of Eden. This promise was God's declaration of war (Genesis 3:15). The barrenness of Sarah and Rebekah was no accident but an attempt to foil the seed of the women being born (Genesis 15:2). In (Genesis 25:21) Isaac prayed to the Lord for his wife, because she was barren. The LORD heard him, and Rebekah his wife conceived. Pharaoh was moved in an attempt to destroy the nation of Israel and so prevent Jesus from being born (Exodus 1:22). Jesus came through the family line of King David. Athaliah tried to destroy the royal line (2 Chronicles 22:10). There was a plot by Haman in Esther's time to exterminate all the Jewish people (Esther 3:13).

Even as Jesus was born, Satan lay in wait to destroy Him. Herod's slaying of the babies in the Bethlehem area was evidence of this (Matthew 2:16). Of course, at the cross, Satan was still trying to destroy the child. Consider Satan entering Judas Iscariot (John 13:27). Did Satan get a glimpse of the terrible mistake he made and so moved people to urge that Jesus would come down from the cross (Mark 15:30)? Satan was finished when Jesus died (John 19:30).

The Dragon

3. And there was seen another sign in the heaven: and behold a great fiery red dragon, having seven heads and ten horns, and upon his heads seven crowns. 4. And his tail drags a third part of the stars of heaven, and he cast them to the earth: and the dragon stood before the woman the one about to give birth, that when she gives birth, he might devour her child. 5. And she bore a male son, who is about to shepherd all the nations with an iron sceptre: and her child was snatched away to God, and his throne. 6. And the woman fled into the desert, where she has a place having been prepared from God, that they might feed her a thousand two hundred and sixty days. (Revelation 12:3-6)

Just so there is no doubt, the prophecy here identifies Satan with the dragon (Revelation 12:9). The Bible links red with sin (Isaiah 1:18). Red also relates to blood, bloodshed and murder (2 Kings 3:22). Red is a feature of Esau who sold his birthright (Genesis 25:30). So, Satan portrayed as red displays his sin, murder and the forsaking of his high position.

The stars of heaven are used to speak of angels (Job 38:7). God first created the heavens and the earth (Genesis 1:1). The word create means calling into being without the aid of pre-existing matter. Rabbi Nachman declares that there is no other word to express production out of nothing. We read, "the earth without form and void" (Genesis 1:2). Fuest defines 'without form' as ruin or desolation. God did not create a desolate ruin. God did not create chaos from which the heavens and the earth formed. Created chaos is a pagan idea (Isaiah 45:18). The earth became ruined when Satan rebelled (Isaiah 14:12-17). Jesus referred to this when He said He saw Satan fall like lightning from heaven (Luke 10:18). When Satan (Lucifer) rebelled against God, he took with him a third of the angels of heaven. This rebellion is referred to as his tail pulling down a third part of the stars of heaven. These are the angels linked with the devil and his angels when they are cast down (Ezekiel 28:13-17). After Satan fell, God had to make the earth (Genesis 1:31). The word 'make' means to fashion or prepare out of existing material (Pember, 1976, pp. 27-73). So God created the heavens and the earth at some unspecified point in the past (Genesis 1:1), they were ruined when Satan fell (Genesis 1:2) but were remade in six days (Genesis 1:3-31).

Satan is the accuser of the brethren. Satan means the accuser. We see him accusing Job (Job 1:9-11) and (Job 2:4-5). Satan accused Joshua the High Priest (Zechariah 3:1-5). Christians are not to come under the condemnation of the Devil (1 Timothy 3:6). There is no condemnation if we live according to the Spirit and not the flesh (Romans 8:1).

Satan appears as having seven heads, ten horns, and seven crowns. Heads speak of rule and authority (Deuteronomy 28:13). Horns talk of power (1 Samuel 2:10). Crowns also emphasise control. Here the word is diadem. Diadem forms from two words: Dia 'because of or through', Deo 'bind or tie'. Persian rulers used a blue band marked with white to tie the turban or tiara.

Seven is the number of fullness. For example, a seven-fold sprinkling on the Day of Atonement marking a perfect fullness of cleansing (Leviticus 16:4-19).

Ten is the number of perfect order. For example, consider the perfection of the Lord's prayer with its ten clauses.

A flood of water comes out of the serpent's mouth (Revelation 12:15). Water can speak of words (Ephesians 5:25-26). However, the words of Satan are lies, and he deceives the nations and stirs them up against the Jewish people and the godly (Revelation 20:3). The earth swallows the flood. There will be people on earth who will help Israel at that time. It is these who are the ones judged to be the sheep when Jesus returns and rewarded at the start of the Millennium (Matthew 25:34–36)

Michael

7. And war happened in the heaven: Michael and his angels waged war against the dragon: and the dragon warred and his angels, 8. And they were not strong enough: nor was a place found for them anymore in the heaven. 9. And the great dragon was thrown down, the ancient snake, the one being called Enemy and Satan, the world-deceiver: he was thrown to the earth, and his angels were thrown down with him. 10. And I heard a great voice saying in the heaven, Now has come the salvation, and the power, and the kingdom of our God, and the authority of his Christ: because the accuser of our brothers has been thrown down, the one accusing them before our God day and night. 11. And they conquered him because of the blood of the Lamb, and because of the word of their witness: and they loved not their life as far as death. 12. Because of this rejoice, the heavens and the ones pitching a tent in them. Woe to the ones inhabiting the earth and the sea, because the devil has gone down to you having great anger, knowing that he has a little time. 13. And when the dragon saw that he had been cast down to the earth, he persecuted the women who had born the male child. 14. And two wings of the great eagle were given to the woman, that she might fly into the desert to her place, where she is fed there a time, and times, and half a time, from the face of the snake. 15. And the snake threw after the woman out of his mouth water as a river, that she might be swept away. 16. And the earth helped the woman, and the earth opened its mouth and swallowed the river which the dragon threw out of his mouth. 17. And the dragon was angry at the woman and departed to make war with the rest of her seed, the ones keeping the commands of God and having the witness of Jesus Christ. (Revelation 12:7-17)

Michael is a powerful heavenly prince one of the chief princes who is involved in warfare in heavenly places (Daniel 10:13). Michael particularly associates with the nation of Israel (Daniel 10:21). He will be active in defence of Israel in the last days (Daniel 12:1). This great time of tribulation is directly linked to Michael casting down Satan. Moreover, we see Michael contending with Satan at other points (Jude 1:9). Michael is an archangel. The word archangel means chief angel. The Greek for 'arch' means to be first in rank. We also see that there is a ranking of angels.

Revelation 13

The Antichrist

The word antichrist is often used when speaking of events during the Tribulation. The word does not occur in Revelation. It is only used four times by John in two of his epistles (1 John 2:18, 22, 4:3, 2 John 1:7). The word literally means an opponent of Christ. John uses it in two senses. He talks of many antichrists referring to those who oppose Christ by denying He is God and that He came born in a physical body. He also refers to one individual who will come in the last time. In Revelation 13 we are shown two opponents of Christ and there has been much debate as to which is the antichrist. Both oppose Christ but in different ways, so both are antichrists. Paul talks of a man of sin being revealed who sits in the temple of God being worshipped (2 Thessalonians 2:3, 4). As we will see below this corresponds to the first beast from the sea. People normally associate him with the specific antichrist that John mentions in his epistles. Revelation also refers to the beast from the sea simply as the beast (Revelation 19:20) and the beast from the land as the false prophet (Revelation 20:10).

The Beast from the Sea

1. And he stood upon the sand of the sea. And I saw coming up out of the sea a wild animal, having seven heads and ten horns, and upon his horns ten crowns, and upon his heads blasphemous names. 2. And the wild animal which I saw was like a leopard, and his feet as a bear and his mouth as a mouth of a lion: and the dragon gave to him his power, and his throne, and great authority. 3. And I saw one of his heads having been slain to death: and the plague of his death had been healed: and the whole earth was filled with wonder after the wild animal. 4. And they worshipped the dragon which had given authority to the wild animal: and they worshipped the wild animal, saying, Who is like the wild animal? Who is able to wage war with him? 5. And a mouth was given to him speaking great things and blasphemies: and authority was given him to do forty-two months. 6. And he opened his mouth into a blasphemy towards God, to blaspheme his name, and his tent, and the ones pitching a tent in the heaven. 7. And it was given to him to make war with the saints, and to conquer them: and authority was given to him over every tribe, and people, and tongue, and nation. 8. And they will worship him all the ones dwelling upon the earth, of whom the names have not been written in the book of life of the Lamb having been slain from the foundation of the world. 9. If anyone has an ear, let him hear. 10. If anyone brings together captives into captivity he goes away: if anyone will kill with a sword, it is necessary for him with a sword to be killed. In this way is the endurance and faith of the saints. (Revelation 13:1-10)

Both a kingdom and a ruler are here depicted. Scripture sometimes links the two, for example (Daniel 2:31-45) speaks of Nebuchadnezzar. God gave him world authority. From this passage, we also see three kingdoms rising up after Nebuchadnezzar with world rule passing to them. These were Medo–Persia, Greece and Rome. Looking at the imagery of the beast mentioned in (Revelation 13), we see all four elements of the representation used in Daniel for these world-ruling kingdoms (Daniel 7:3-7).

This first beast in Revelation then will be a world-ruling empire with an emperor. Since, as we have seen, there was a breach of promise between the end of Daniels sixty-ninth week and the beginning of Daniels seventieth week. The Roman Empire that existed at the rejection of Christ will reappear as a western empire during the final seven-year period. It is this beast and its ruler, which is being spoken of here.

The dragon stood upon the sand of the sea and saw a beast rise up out of the sea (Revelation 13:1). Sand speaks of countless multitudes, (Genesis 32:12). The sea speaks of the restless wicked, (Isaiah 57:20). This ruler's empire is coming from the multitudes of the restless wicked of the earth.

It had seven heads, ten horns and ten crowns upon his horns (Revelation 13:1). Compare this to the description of the dragon in (Revelation 12:3) with seven heads, ten horns and seven crowns upon his heads. We see the Devil energising the ruler, and the kingdom described here. Comparing this description with (Daniel 7:19-25) this territory will consist of a federation of ten countries. The seven heads also refer to seven types of government. Up to John, there were five forms of government in the Roman Empire. These were: kings, consuls, dictators, decemvir and military tribunals. Current with John was the sixth type of government, imperial, initiated by Julius Caesar. The final kind of state is yet to be. This indicates that this beast will be a revived Roman or Western Empire (Revelation 17:10-13).

The beast looked like a leopard, with bear's feet, and the mouth of a lion (Revelation 12:2). As we have seen, the great kingdoms of the Gentiles in (Daniel 7) manifest in these terms. The beast in Revelation then is the culmination of Gentile power.

The leopard speaks of unrepentant evildoers (Jeremiah 13:23).

A bear compares to a fool in his folly (Proverbs 17:12).

Lions and bears together were sheep stealers and slayers (1 Samuel 17:34). A wicked ruler over a poor/helpless people features the characters of a lion and a bear (Proverbs 28:15).

Thus, we see the ethos of this kingdom and its ruler.

The beast had a wounded head that was healed (Revelation 13:3). Satan ever counterfeits the works and ways of God. We see here a counterfeiting of the resurrection (2 Corinthians 11:14). The reviving of this empire from what had collapsed and passed away may also be here. The Roman Empire lasted for 900 years. For centuries, it has been lost from the empires of men.

The world worships the beast and the dragon behind it (Revelation 13:4). Rulers have ever wanted their followers to deify them. This has been a trait through history. The sway this ruler will have over people will be as great or greater than any other ruler. For some years before Hitler's defeat, many worshipped him. We are to worship God and not another (John 4:23, 24). It was standard practice to deify Roman Emperors. Much of the Christian persecution in the Roman Empire came from the fact that they would not worship the Emperors.

The beast speaks great things and blasphemies (Revelation 13:5, 6). The wicked are forever boasting and talk to make themselves look good in the eyes of others (Psalm 94:3-6). Satan's real power over men has always involved words, lies and deceit. The end times will see the servants of Satan lying to deceive (1 Timothy 4:1, 2). Satan's deception is foretold explicitly in Daniel (Daniel 7:8).

He makes war with the saints and overcomes them (Revelation 13:7). Daniel prophesies that this will be through a process of wearing them out (Daniel 7:25).

Patience is therefore required of the godly when resisting this beast (Revelation 13:10). Patience is not being able to stand quietly in a queue, in true British fashion. Instead, it means to 'stay under' whatever burden or oppression comes our way when we are required to be faithful to God (James 5:7, 8).

The Beast out of the Earth

11. And I saw another wild animal coming up out of the land, and he was having two horns like a lamb, and he was speaking as a dragon. 12. And all the authority of the first wild animal he is doing before him, and he makes the land and the ones dwelling in it to worship the first wild animal whose plague of death had been healed. 13. And he does great signs, that he might even make fire to come down out of the heaven to the land before men. 14. And he leads astray the ones dwelling upon the land because of the signs which he was given to do before the wild animal: saying to the ones dwelling upon the land, to make an image of the wild animal, which has the plague of the sword and has lived. 15. And it was given to him to give breath to the image of the wild animal, that also the image of the wild animal might speak and might make as many as would not worship the image of the wild animal to be killed. 16. And he makes all, the small and the great, also the rich and the poor, and the free and the slave, that he might give to them a mark upon their right hand, or upon their foreheads: 17. And that no one should be able to buy or sell, unless the one having the mark or the name of the wild animal, or the number of his name. 18. In this way is wisdom. The one having understanding let him count the number of the wild animal: for it is the number of a man: and the number is six hundred and sixty-six.
(Revelation 13:11-18)

This is a false shepherd that the nation Israel will trust in (Zechariah 11:15–17).

He comes up out of the earth (Revelation 13:11) The Old Testament when speaking of the land points to the land of Israel. This is a trait that occurs again and again, (Daniel 8:9). The little horn of (Daniel 8) is the second beast, but the little horn of (Daniel 7) is the first beast. A very detailed prophecy in (Daniel 11) looks at the kings of the north and the south. They are north and south of the land of Israel. This second beast comes from the land of Israel. For him to be a false Messiah received by the Jewish people he would have to be a Jew from the land. Some people think he will come from the tribe of Dan because of the prophecy of Israel to his sons (Genesis 49:17-18).

He has two horns like a lamb (Revelation 13:11). He is likened unto a lamb, as a counterfeit of Christ the Lamb, but speaks like a dragon, the symbol of Satan.

He causes the world to worship the first beast (Revelation 13:12). This is counterfeiting Jesus glorifying the Father (Daniel 11:36-39)

He does great wonders (Revelation 13:13, 14). Counterfeiting miracles will mark the end times (2 Thessalonians 2:6-12).

He causes an image of the first beast to be set up and worshipped (Revelation 13:14, 15). This false prophet will set up an image in a temple that will be in Jerusalem (Daniel 11:31), (Daniel 12:11) and (Matthew 24:15).

The number of the second beast is 666 (Revelation 13:18). This was the secret symbol of the ancient pagan mysteries connected with worshipping the Devil.

Gematria is the ancient world's way of counting using their alphabets. Any word can be a number in the original Biblical languages. This is not the same as something that recently has been talked about called 'Bible Code.'

Sigma, used instead of the sixth letter of the Greek alphabet, stands for the number six. Moreover, a particular form of the letter sigma is used which is called stigma. We get our word stigma from it. This was a mark or brand burnt into slaves, cattle or soldiers. Those who receive the mark of the beast become the slaves, cattle and soldiers of this evil Satanic kingdom.

Three evil men link to 666.

1. (1 Samuel 17:4-7) Goliath was six cubits high, had six pieces of armour and his iron spearhead weighed 600 shekels.

2. (Daniel 3:1) Nebuchadnezzar's image was 60 cubits high, six cubits broad and was worshipped with six specified instruments.

3. The third will be the beast from the land (Revelation 13:11–18).

Contrast the Gematria counted from the name of Jesus, which is 888.

In (Revelation 12 and 13) we see the unholy trinity, the counterfeit of the true Trinity, being set up on earth.

- The dragon counterfeiting the Holy Spirit

- The first beast imitating God, the Father

- The second beast setting himself up as a false Christ

Revelation 14

1. And I saw, and behold, a Lamb having stood upon Mount Zion, and with him one hundred and forty-four thousand, having the name of his father having been written upon their foreheads. 2. And I heard a voice out of the heaven, as a voice of many waters, and as a voice of great thunder: and I heard the voice of harpists playing their harps. 3. And they sang as it were a new song before the throne, and before the four living beings, and the elders: and no one was able to learn the song, except the hundred and forty-four thousand the ones having been purchased from the earth. 4. These are the ones not having been defiled with women: for they are virgins. These are the ones following the Lamb wherever he may go. These have been bought from men, firstfruits to God and to the Lamb. 5. And in their mouth was not found deceit: for they are blameless before the throne of God. (Revelation 14:1-5)

The Lamb on Mount Zion

This is the Lord Jesus, the true Lamb of God (John 1:36). Contrast Him with the beast from the land, who looked like a lamb but spoke like a dragon (Revelation 13:11).

In Revelation 12 we saw the Lord Jesus Christ depicted as the child. The image of the child pointed to His birth death, resurrection and ascension. The Lamb in Revelation 14 sees Him standing on Mount Zion.

Zion in the Bible is a literal place. People have taken a spiritual application from this, and that is appropriate. Similarly, people have made a spiritual application from Jerusalem, which is also a physical place. Both the literal and the spiritual go together. The literal foreshadows spiritual realities and considering both are important.

Zion was a stronghold within the city of Jerusalem, which David captured (2 Samuel 5:7). One day, David's most significant descendant will also win the stronghold of Zion again. He will then stand upon this place when He returns.

We have already seen whom the 144,000 are who will stand with Him. These are in Revelation 7. They are the faithful from the nation of Israel who remains true to God in the difficult last seven years before the Lord Jesus returns.

Again, and again in Revelation, we observe that there will be a victorious people of God despite the attempts by Satan to set up his own kingdom. It is these people who will ascend Zion the hill of the Lord. Their qualities are mentioned here, namely their purity, and right speaking. Psalm 24 speaks of the return of Jesus to the city of Jerusalem and the hill of Zion. It also speaks of those qualities of the faithful who will stand with him.

Angelic Messages

A series of angelic messages are given in this chapter proclaiming what is about to happen in the second half of the Tribulation.

The Everlasting Gospel Preached

6. And I saw another angel flying in mid-heaven, having the eternal good news to proclaim to the ones dwelling upon the earth, and to every nation, and tribe, and tongue, and people. 7. Saying in a great voice, Fear God, and give to him glory: because the hour of his judgement has come: and worship the one having made the heaven, and the earth, and the sea, and the springs of waters. (Revelation 14:6, 7)

An angel is flying in midheaven which is the position in the sky of the sun at its highest point during the day. This angel will be visible to all. At this point, Michael has forced the Satanic powers out of the heavenly realms (Revelation 12:9), and so this angel will move unopposed. Satan has directly opposed angelic ministry on occasions. An example of this was when an angel was sent in response to Daniel's prayers but delayed for three weeks because of a spiritual being called the prince of the Persian kingdom (Daniel 10:13).

The word angel means messenger, and in this instance, we see an angelic messenger with the eternal gospel as his message. Before the judgement of God falls on the sins of mankind, all will hear the good news about forgiveness through the Lord Jesus Christ. The gospel proclaimed before the end comes was foretold by Jesus when He was answering the disciples' questions about the end of the age (Matthew 24:14). God in His love and mercy gives every opportunity for people to find forgiveness. This mercy means that when judgement falls men will not be able to use the excuse that they did not know. Those who face God's punishment will do so in the full knowledge that they rejected the Lord Jesus Christ (Romans 1:18, 19).

The people of the earth will see and hear an angel proclaiming the gospel at this desperate time. At key points in history, God has sent angels with messages to men. When Jesus was born, the shepherds saw angels (Luke 2:8-14). Jesus tells a story of a rich man being in hell. The rich man wanted someone to come from the dead to warn his five brothers not to make the mistake he did. He was told even if someone came from the dead they would not believe. Sadly, many people have not believed though Jesus rose from the dead and returned to the earth, perhaps then an angel can persuade men? God will not be accused of leaving any stone unturned in seeking to save men from eternal punishment.

How in practice does angelic evangelism work? We are used to the church having been commissioned to proclaim the gospel (Mark 16:15). The church will have been taken to be with the Lord before the time of judgement begins, and the way in which things work seems are more in keeping with the Old Testament. This change makes sense since God will once again be dealing with the Jewish people and the Gentiles distinctly. Moses received the Law mediated by angels (Galatians 3:19). It was on this basis that he ministered. In the first half of the Tribulation, there will be two witnesses and many other people proclaiming the good news (Revelation 11:1-14, 12:11). Given how much harder it will be to proclaim the Gospel in the second half of the Tribulation, through this angel we see part of the spiritual mechanism by which this is happening. Even at this time angels are described as ministering spirits to those who are heirs of salvation (Hebrews 1:14). It has yet to be revealed to us the part angels play for God in the spreading of the gospel.

The good news of Jesus Christ has been proclaimed and will be for all eternity. God purposed Jesus' sacrifice from the beginning (Revelation 13:8). From the day of Adam's fall the promise of Jesus' coming as Saviour and deliverer was given (Genesis 3:15). The good news has been announced since the fall of man.

This declaration is in the Old Testament prophetically:

- Through symbolic acts, for example, God clothing Adam and Eve with animal skins. An animal had to die, and blood spilt. The word for 'clothe' is often translated 'atone' (Genesis 3:21).

- Through people's lives, for example, God provided a ram instead of Isaac for Abraham to sacrifice. In the same way, Jesus took the place of every man upon the cross (Genesis 22:13).

- Through the law, for example, the scapegoat on the Day of Atonement carried the nations transgressions away (Leviticus 16:21, 22).

- Through the prophets, for example, Isaiah prophesied in detail about the crucifixion (Isaiah 53:5).

- Through enactments of the lives of the prophets, for example, Daniel in the lion's den is a picture of the death and resurrection of Jesus (Daniel 6:20-22).

In the New Testament:

- The church has been commissioned to proclaim the good news of Jesus Christ (Mark 16:15, 16).

- The end will not come without the preaching of the gospel throughout the earth by the Tribulation saints (Matthew 24:14).

- Throughout eternity the people of God will show to all the salvation they have received through Christ (1 Peter 2:9).

The good news that the angel proclaims is summed up in four points. Do we declare these four points when we preach the good news? There seems to be much that is lacking from so many modern 'gospel' messages.

Fear the Lord

The fear of the Lord is an essential part of the message of the good news. Unfortunately, people have a distorted view of what this means. Many have a medieval idea of torture and terror which our present culture has created to turn people away from something that is both life-giving and good. I fear to put my hand into a fire because it will hurt me which is a healthy fear that protects me from pain and trauma. The fear of God is like this. It is something that is wholesome and life-bringing. It does not stress people out or traumatise them. The Bible says that the fear of the Lord is pure (Psalm 19:9). Moreover, the fear of the Lord is the beginning of wisdom (Proverbs 9:10). A realisation of who God is and the importance of preparing to meet Him is an excellent and essential aspect of living a joyful life.

Give Him glory

Achan sinned against the Lord when he took some plunder that belonged to the Lord after the destruction of Jericho (Joshua 7:21). His sin resulted in Israel losing a battle and some of the Israelites dying. Joshua told him to confess his sin and acknowledge his crime. The expression Joshua used was 'give glory to the Lord' (Joshua 7:19). One aspect of giving glory to God is to admit what He says about us is correct and respond to Him in the light of this. In other words, we need to acknowledge our wrongdoing and seek God's forgiveness.

For the hour of His judgement has come.

Many Christians are reluctant to mention the coming judgement of God when seeking to witness to others. Jesus spoke more about judgement than anyone else in the New Testament. It is essential that people hear so that they might avoid eternal damnation. If we saw someone running towards a cliff and did not stop them, others would condemn us if the runner fell to their death. Why do we think it is acceptable not to warn people of the coming judgement?

Worship Him

The root meaning of the word worship conveys the idea of humbling ourselves before the greatness of God. One word used comes from a dog licking its master's hand. Since we have been created by God and owe our ongoing existence to Him, our attitude should be one of humility, love and devotion to Him.

Babylon is Fallen

8. And another angel followed, saying, Fallen, fallen Babylon the great city, because of the wine of the anger of her sexual immorality she has given a drink to all nations. (Revelation 14:8)

Alexander the Great destroyed Babylon in 330 BC. He intended to rebuild but his early death cut this short. Although the site remained inhabited, it continued to decline. A clay tablet about 10 B.C. contains its last mention. It now exists as a mound passed by the Baghdad to Bassorah railway line.

The book of Revelation here declares the fall of Babylon and Revelation 17 to 19 majors about the fall. How can this be since the city has already fallen? It would seem that at some point the city of Babylon will be rebuilt and become a major world city again. Some people would quote (Jeremiah 50:39) where it says that Babylon shall no more be inhabited forever. They would argue that Babylon was overthrown and as this scripture has been fulfilled, it cannot be rebuilt. However, we see an example here of prophecy having some partial fulfilments before a perfect and final fulfilment. The previous occasions where Babylon fell foreshadow a much greater spectacular fall. That a literal city is spoken of is clear because many stand far off and witness its destruction (Revelation 18:9, 10).

In scripture, Babylon is more than a place; it is a world system that is contrary to the Kingdom of God. Babylon, the city from ancient times, has birthed a culture that has poisoned the earth. It is a culture that permeates our lives both inside and outside the church organisations we have. As a culture, we are unaware of it and so usually do not challenge it because we think it is the way things should be. A piece of knowledge that we are not aware we have is dangerous because we do not critically evaluate it to see if the understanding is correct or beneficial.

It began shortly after the flood with a renewed rebellion against God that centred around Babel and Nimrod (Genesis 11:1-9). The name Babel is the original form of the name Babylon. From this rebellion, all the systems of the world that we are so familiar with began.

History and archaeology have a lot of details about this time that is helpful to know in studying about Babylon in the scriptures. A detailed account of this is given by (Hislop, 1975). This book though published in 1916 is still readily available.

Five main areas of this world system were established after the flood.

1. Empire: the tendency for men to set up kingdoms through war and conquest. With empire comes rulers or emperors and the idea of men being in hierarchies over other men.

2. Commerce: the systems of trade and money came into being from this rebellion. Our current fiscal policies are on the same foundation as Babel.

3. Religion: Nimrod was worshipped as a god. The whole idolatrous system of religion began from this root. Many of the names of the gods are linked linguistically to the chief characters living at that time, namely Cush, the grandson of Noah, Nimrod his son and Nimrod's wife, Semiramis.

4. The Mysteries: There was a whole system of knowledge that was only for the initiated. These things were hidden, and our word 'occult' means hidden. The world's systems of secret societies and practices began in Babylon.

5. Immorality: Linked with the whole system was appalling moral uncleanness. The world has become full of this filth.

The beautiful thing about Jesus' return is that this whole evil system will be cast down and destroyed.

The Wrath of God Poured Out

9. And a third angel followed them, saying in a great voice, If anyone worships the wild animal and his image, and receives a mark upon his forehead, or upon his hand, 10. Even he will drink of the wine of the anger of God, having been mixed untempered in the cup of his anger, and he will be tormented in fire and sulphur before the holy angels, and before the Lamb: 11. And the smoke of their torment rises into ages of ages: and they have not rest day and night, the one worshipping the wild animal and his image, and if anyone receives the mark of his name. 12. In this way is the endurance of the saints: in this way are the ones keeping the commandments of God, and the faith of Jesus. (Revelation 14:9-12)

The Ark of the Covenant in the Old Testament Tabernacle was a picture of God. The ark consisted of two parts, a box containing the tablets of stone on which the Ten Commandments were written, and a lid called the mercy seat. The presence of God dwelt immediately above the Ark of the Covenant (Exodus 25:10-22). One of the things that this demonstrates is that God is both just and merciful. In the mercy seat meeting the box containing the law, we see mercy and judgement met together in God (Psalm 85:10). One of the themes of Revelation is the justice of God.

In the Tribulation, it will be very hard not to worship the beast or receive his mark. Those who rebel will not be able to buy or sell. They will face torture and death. The path of following God will be very hard at this time. It will be so tempting to receive the mark and bow to the image. It will be important for those who remain faithful to God to consider the alternative. Although initially, it may be more comfortable to receive the mark of the beast the result will be eternal torment.

It was the custom to add water to wine when drinking in Bible times. Undiluted, unmixed wine is used to describe the nature of God's anger. God is perfect in every way. When He is angry, He is perfectly angry. We associate anger and other so-called 'negative' emotions with wrongdoing. These emotions are neither right nor wrong. God can function in any emotion in a right way. We can often operate emotionally in wrong directions. When God is angry, it is appropriate and necessary. God is going to be angry with those who receive the mark of the beast forever. God is eternal, and His punishment for sin will be everlasting.

The punishment of wrongdoers who have not trusted in Jesus for forgiveness will be in the presence of God and the angels. The idea that the Lake of Fire is a place where God is not is incorrect. There is no place where people can go to escape the presence of God (Psalm 139:7, 8). I can think of no more uncomfortable and shameful place to be than before God with sin unforgiven. Isaiah in encountering God's presence and holiness could not easily cope and needed cleansing from God (Isaiah 6:5). Well is this place depicted as a place of eternal burning. Physically a burn is a very painful wound, how much more the undiluted anger of God against unforgiven sin (Mark 9:48).

The Voice from Heaven and the Spirits Response

13. And I heard a voice out of the heaven saying to me, Write, Blessed the dead, the ones in the Lord dying from now: Yes, says the Spirit, that they might rest from their troubles: but their works follow after them. (Revelation 14:13)

The Bible has a lot to say about perseverance. The word persevere means to remain under pressure. An example of this would be the soldier on the front line of an ancient army when the enemy cavalry is charging towards them. To persevere is to stand the ground and not run away. We continue because God enables us to persist. It is essential to remain true to Jesus because that is the mark of true discipleship. If it is true in our days, it will also be right in the Tribulation. There is a reward for being faithful in difficulties (James 1:12). Those who die in the Tribulation, having remained faithful to the Lord Jesus, will receive a high reward. We see this company in heaven (Revelation 7:9-17). The Holy Spirit affirms what the voice from heaven is saying and underlines the importance of remembering this. When God repeats Himself, it is because something is sure and will soon happen (Genesis 41:32).

The Grain Harvest

14. And I saw, and behold, a white cloud, and upon the cloud sitting one like the Son of Man, having upon his head a victor's crown of gold, and in his hand a sharp sickle. 15. And another angel came out of the inner shrine of the temple, crying in a great voice to the one sitting upon the cloud, Send your sickle and reap: because the harvest of the earth has dried up. 16. And the one sitting upon the cloud threw his sickle upon the earth: and the earth was reaped. (Revelation 14:14-16)

The son of man is none other than the Lord Jesus Christ. He is often referred to by this title. There are eighty-five times He is mentioned as the Son of Man in the New Testament (Matthew 8:20). The cloud is always linked to the glory and presence of God (Matthew 17:5). When Jesus returns to judge the world, He is connected to the cloud (Matthew 24:30). The kind of crown Jesus is wearing is a victor's crown similar to those worn by victorious generals in victory parades or athletes who won in the Olympic games. Jesus is the triumphant and victorious one. He is coming as the overcomer who has triumphed over all His enemies (Ephesians 4:8). Jesus spoke of the end of the age and the coming judgment as a time of harvest (Matthew 13:40-42). John the Baptist introduced Jesus as the one who collects in the crop (Matthew 3:12). Jesus is pictured here as someone coming and scything down His enemies just as wheat is harvested which is a fitting introduction to the seven bowl judgements that are in (Revelation 15 and 16). They give more details of this scything that will take place. The kind of ripeness that communicated in the word used here is that of the overripe, something which has become rotten, dried up or wasted away.

The Grape Harvest

17. And another angel came out of the inner shrine of the temple in the heaven, having also himself a sharp sickle. 18. And another angel came out of the altar, having authority over the fire: and he called with a great shout to the one having the sharp sickle, Send your sharp sickle and gather the bunches of grapes of the vineyard of the earth: because its grapes ripened. 19. And the angel threw his sickle into the earth, and he gathered the vineyard of the earth, and he threw it into the great winepress of the anger of God. 20. And the winepress was trampled outside of the city, and blood came out of the winepress, as far as the bridles of the horses, for one thousand six hundred stadia. (Revelation 14:17-20)

The collecting of the grapes for the winepress is referring to the final assembly of the nations against Jesus when He returns at Armageddon. The grapes will be in the winepress, and they will be trodden out (Revelation 14:18-20). When the Lord Jesus comes, He will make war against His enemies (Revelation 19:11-21). Their blood will be shed and is pictured as the Lord Jesus trampling out grapes in a winepress (Isaiah 63:3-4). The bloodshed will run for 1600 furlongs which is 200 miles or the length of the land of Israel.

Revelation 15

1. And I saw another sign in heaven, great and wonderful, seven angels, having the seven last plagues: because in them the anger of God has been fulfilled. (Revelation 15:1)

The last seven plagues end with the return of Jesus. They take place during the Tribulation and within the last trumpet sounded by the seventh angel (Revelation 11:15-19). They fit within the seven seals and trumpets. The seventh trumpet sounds for many days (Revelation 10:7). Another example of an extended trumpet sounding happened when Moses was on Mount Sinai (Exodus 19:13, 16, 19). We know that Israel flees into the wilderness in the middle of the Tribulation (Revelation 12:14, Matthew 24:15-21). The bowls are poured out after this event (Revelation 16).

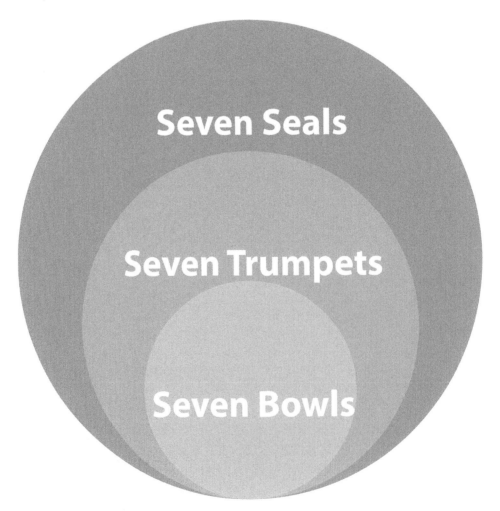

The Seven Bowls

Before the bowls of God's anger are poured out on the earth, we again witness the reassuring vision of the people of God coming through this time victorious. The book of Revelation keeps reminding us that the people of God will triumph. We get a vision of the triumph before we see what they triumph over. Remember the images of Revelation are not always in chronological order.

2. And I saw as it were a sea made of glass having been mixed with fire: and the ones overcoming the wild animal, and over his image, and over his mark, and over the number of his name, having stood upon the sea of glass, having the harps of God. 3. And they sing the song of Moses the servant of God, and the song of the Lamb, saying, Great and wonderful are your works, Lord God Almighty, right and true are your ways, King of the saints. 4. Who absolutely would not fear you, Lord, and glorify your name? because only you are holy: that all the nations will come and will worship before you: because your righteous acts were made known. (Revelation 15:2-4)

They stand on a sea of glass mingled with fire

Before the throne of God, which is His judgement seat, stands an expansive pavement. This pavement is also called a sea of glass (Revelation 4:6). The throne of a ruler whether a king or governor often was also a judgement seat from which sentencing happened either condemning or vindicating those standing before it. Often before these thrones were pavements which served the purpose of allowing both those on trial before the king and witnesses to assemble before the throne. Pilate had such a judgement seat and pavement. The pavement was known as Gabbatha (John 19:3). Here Jesus was falsely accused and unrighteously condemned.

In the sea of glass, we learn important lessons regarding the judgement of God and those who stand before the throne.

Moses and the elders of Israel stood before that place (Exodus 24:9-11). Moses and the elders were not destroyed, eating and drinking in God's presence. They stood in the position of judgement, uncondemned. The righteous stand by grace through Jesus but the wicked cannot remain in that place without being found guilty (Psalm 1:5).

We see the sea of glass again in Ezekiel's vision of God (Ezekiel 1:22). It is: -

An expanse
In other words, an extended surface. The place of judgement before God is big enough for all to stand and every thought and action presented.

Awesome
The root of this word is to fear. The judgement pavement of God is a place to be feared. It is a serious thing to stand before God in judgement.

Gleaming
The word refers to the eye and the visible. The all-seeing eyes of God see everything in that place. There can be no hiding or secrets from God.

Crystalline (Clear)

God judges everything and all is made clear. There is no confusion or lies. All actions display for what they are. People are known thoroughly, and every issue weighed aright.

In (Revelation 4:6) there are multitudes of witnesses present. The judgement of God is a public thing. The court of God is in public. All see both the justification of the righteous and the condemnation of the wicked.

The victorious people of God stand before the Lord. Fire is within the sea is indicating God is a God of judgement (Hebrews 12:29). All that is worthless is burned up, but all that is good is refined and will be treasured forever.

When Israel crossed the Red Sea (Exodus 14), a picture of the two outcomes of the judgement of God was displayed. The Israelites represent the redeemed people of God who pass through the sea unharmed. Pharaoh and his chariots are like the wicked who God overcame and overthrew when they encountered the sea.

It is no coincidence, therefore, that the Tribulation Saints sing the song of Moses with harps, (Revelation 15:3). The song of Moses was sung by Israel when they had victory over Pharaoh and his chariots at the Red Sea (Exodus 15:1–11). So here we see the saints singing victoriously after their enemies have been judged and defeated by the Lord. Harps are symbols of joy. When the children of Israel had no happiness, they hung their harps on the willows (Psalm 137:2, 3). These victorious saints are singing with joy before the throne of God.

The Tribulation Saints overcame three things

The Beast energised by Satan, (Revelation 13:2)

Satan will particularly want to wear down and destroy the righteous in the Tribulation, (Daniel 7:25).

The Beast's Image (Revelation 13:14).

Just as Nebuchadnezzar threw Shadrach, Meshach and Abed-nego into a fiery furnace (Daniel 2) for not bowing down to an image he created, so many of the Tribulation Saints will be killed for not bowing down.

The Number of his Name which is 666 (Revelation 13:18)

It will not be possible to buy or sell without this number branded upon either the head or arm. The Tribulation Saints will have endured starvation and intense pressure to tempt them to receive this mark (Revelation 13:17).

All who overcome in God, overcome in three areas. In the case of Jesus, this was in three temptations (Matthew 4:1-11). More generally, the people of God who have overcome, overcome the lust of the flesh, the desire of the eyes and the pride of life (1 John 2:16).

Comparing different overcomers, we see: -

The lust of the flesh	Jesus tempted to turn stones into bread	Receiving the number of the Beast to purchase food
The lust of the eyes	Satan promising Jesus the kingdoms of the world if He worshipped	Worshipping the image of the Beast
The pride of life	The temptation to prove Jesus was the Son of God by throwing Himself off the Temple	The Beast energised by Satan in all his pride

The Scene Now Focuses on the Judgement of God

5. And after these things, I saw, and behold, the inner shrine of the temple was opened the tent of the witness in heaven: 6. And the seven angels having the seven plagues came out of the inner shrine of the temple, the ones having been clothed in linen pure and bright and having been wrapped about the breasts with golden belts. 7. And one of the four living beings gave to the seven angels seven gold bowls being full of the anger of God, living into the ages of the ages. 8. And the inner shrine of the temple was filled with smoke from the glory of God and from his power: and no one was able to enter into the inner shrine of the temple until the seven plagues of the seven angels were finished. (Revelation 15:5-8)

A cloud is filling the temple (Revelation 15:8) which is showing that no petition is possible. No plea for mercy is going to be received (Lamentations 3:44).

The word bowls are translated as vials which are shallow cups. These are the same as the bowls and basins used for sacrifice in the Old Testament (Exodus 27:1-3). The nations have rejected the atoning sacrifice of Christ, so they face the wrath of God poured out on the altar of God directed at them.

The bowls correspond closely to the Egyptian plagues, which foretold of this greater judgement and deliverance:

Bowls	Egyptian Plague
1. Boils	6th Plague - Boils (Exodus 9:8)
2. Blood	1st Plague - Blood (Exodus 7:14)
3. Blood	1st Plague – Blood (Exodus 7:14)
4. Scorching Heat	
5. Darkness	9th Plague – Darkness (Exodus 10:21)
6. Frogs	2nd Plague – Frogs (Exodus 8:1)
7. Hail	7th Plague – Hail (Exodus 9:13)

Revelation 16

1. And I heard a great voice out of the inner shrine of the temple, saying, Go away, and pour out the bowls of the anger of God into the earth. (Revelation 16:1)

The people of God prayed that God would render unto their wicked neighbours, "Seven times into their bosom their reproach." God here is responding to the cries of His people and judging His enemies who have reproached Him (Psalm 79:12).

First Bowl

2. And the first came away and poured out his bowl upon the earth: and there came a bad and evil sore into the men having the mark of the wild animal, and the one worshipping his image.
(Revelation 16:2)

Wounds are upon the men who have followed the beast. The word can mean boils. The picture is of ulcers producing pus. One of the consequences of following Satan will be an eruption of the flesh yielding all manner of foul uncleanness. The Bible uses the picture of a discharge of the body to symbolise uncleanness, (Leviticus 15:2). This uncleanness will be manifested by boils physically upon people. They will only be upon people who have received the mark of the beast. The boils will further create hostility toward those who have not received the mark and therefore do not have the boils. Perhaps there is something in the marking process that leads to this infection.

Second Bowl

3. And the second angel poured out his bowl into the sea: and it became blood as a dead man, and every soul living died in the sea. (Revelation 16:3)

The sea becomes the blood as of a dead man. As we have seen, the sea is a picture of the wicked, (Isaiah 57:20). Death is the evildoer's lot both physically and spiritually (James 1:15). The Tribulation is the time when sin will be full-grown and dying results. The impact of every living thing in the sea dying will make life unsustainable upon the earth. The sea dying is one of the reasons why God will cut short the Tribulation otherwise no one would survive (Matthew 24:22). It is salt water life that is the focus of this judgement.

Third Bowl

4. And the third angel poured out his bowl into the rivers and into the springs of waters: and it became blood. 5. And I heard the angel of the waters saying, Righteous, Lord you are, the one being and the one who was and the holy one who will be because you judged these things. 6. Because the blood of the saints and prophets they poured out, and you gave blood to them to drink: for they are worthy. 7. And I heard another out of the altar saying, Yes, Lord God Almighty, true and righteous are your judgements. (Revelation 16:4-7)

The third bowl produces blood in all the drinking waters, the rivers and fountains which is showing that the wicked will now drink of the evil they have done. As sinful man has shed blood so shall his blood be shed (Genesis 9:6). The world is already full of violence and bloodshed but how much more when God's restraint departs. The penalty that God decreed after the flood still stands and is one of the reasons so much blood will be shed by men at the time of judgement.

Fourth Bowl

8. And the fourth angel poured out his bowl upon the sun: and it was given to him to scorch men in fire. 9. And the men were scorched with great heat, and they blasphemed the name of God, the one having authority over the plagues: and they repented not to give him glory. (Revelation 16:8, 9)

The sun quite literally will flare up and scorch men. There appears to be, within the judgements upon the earth, a reshaping of the earth in preparation for the Millennium. The earth before the Flood in Noah's time was very different to what it is now. We can infer some differences by looking at the details of the early chapters of Genesis. There was a great canopy of water surrounding the planet. It was this firmament collapsing upon the earth that caused the rain. It may be that the increase in evaporation from the oceans that would result from the sun scorching in the Tribulation could begin to restore this canopy.

There is a principle of the physical manifesting the spiritual. When Jesus performed miracles, the miracles demonstrated deeper spiritual truths. For example, when Jesus cleansed the leper, it was showing that He could cleanse people from sin. Figuratively, the sun scorching here is not referring to Jesus the Sun of Righteousness. When He arises as the Sun, it will be to bring healing (Malachi 4:2). The sun is a symbol of a ruler (Genesis 1:16). A ruler will arise who will cause the wicked great distress. The sun would appear to be the first beast, the ruler of the western empire. The context is of those who have received the mark of the beast via the prophet of the first beast. On that day, the wicked will be burned up (Malachi 4:1).

Fifth Bowl

10. And the fifth angel poured out his bowl upon the throne of the wild animal: and his kingdom became darkened: and they chewed their tongues out of pain, 11. And they blasphemed the God of heaven out of their pains and their sores, and they repented not of their works. (Revelation 16:10, 11)

Darkness results from this bowl being poured out. The physical manifestation of this demonstrates a deeper spiritual darkness will be upon wicked men at this time (2 Timothy 3:13).

Sixth Bowl

12. And the sixth angel poured out his bowl upon the great river Euphrates: and its water was dried up, that the way of the kings from the rising of the sun might be prepared. 13. And I saw out of the mouth of the dragon, and out of the mouth of the wild animal, and out of the mouth of the false prophet, three unclean spirits like frogs. 14. For they are spirits of demons doing signs, to go out upon the kings of the whole inhabited earth, to gather them to the war of the great day of God the Almighty. 15. Behold, I come as a thief. Blessed the one watching, and keeping his garments, that he might not walk about naked, and they see his shame. 16. And he gathered them into the place being called in Hebrew Armageddon. (Revelation 16:12-16)

Frogs that are evil spirits working miracles deceive the nations into battle. These armies gather that God might pour out His anger upon the nations (Zephaniah 3:8). The Euphrates was the border of the Roman Empire and has been a border throughout history. The drying up of this indicates Eastern armies are moving towards the land of Israel. It is not clear how united the earth will have remained at this point to the beast. Will these armies be marching to support the beast, or will they be moving to fight him?

The site of the battle is Armageddon in the land of Israel. Armageddon is the hill of Megiddo. For the nation of Israel, it marked two great victories and two great disasters.

The two great victories were:

- Barak defeating Sisera (Judges 5:19).

- Gideon overcoming the Midianites (Judges 7:22)

The two great disasters were:

- Saul killed by the Philistines (1 Samuel 31:1-6)

- Josiah murdered by Pharaoh Necho (2 Kings 23:29)

Armageddon will be both, initially, a place of defeat but then of victory for Israel on the day of the Lord.

Seventh Bowl

17. And the seventh angel poured out his bowl into the air: and a great voice came out from the inner shrine of the temple of the heaven, from the throne saying, It has become. 18. And there were voices, and thunders, and lightnings: and a great earthquake happened, such as it had not happened from when men became upon the earth, such a great earthquake. 19. And the great city became split into three parts, and the cities of the nation's fell: and Babylon the great was remembered before God, to give to her the cup of the wine of the rage of his anger. 20. And every island fled, and mountains were not found. 21. And great hail as weighing a talent comes down out of the heaven upon men: men blasphemed God because of the plague of hail: because the plague is itself very great. (Revelation 16:17-21)

On the day that Jesus' feet touch the Mount of Olives, there will be a great earthquake (Zechariah 14:4). The quake will be the sign of a much more significant shaking (Hebrews 12:25-28).

The impact of this earthquake will be massive upon the land of Israel and the rest of the earth. If we take the prophecies of this quake literally, we have a startling reshaping of the continents with the return of Jesus. We are told that the mountain on which the temple stands will be raised as chief of the mountains (Isaiah 2:2). Every valley is lifted up, and every mountain and hill will be made low (Isaiah 40:4). We are looking at a world where Jerusalem will be the highest point on the earth and where the continents are much more level.

Looking at the land of Israel more closely the Mount of Olives will split apart with one part moving northward and the other moving south forming a great valley. The Mediterranean will flow into the Dead Sea with a fall about eight times the height of Niagara (Tatford, 1971, p. 161). If Noah's flood completely reshaped the earth how much more the return of Jesus? Our imagination of what the return of Jesus will look like is probably too small and limited.

Revelation 17

1. And one of the seven angels having the seven bowls came, and spoke with me, saying to me, Come, I will show you the judgement of the great prostitute, the one sitting upon many waters: 2. With whom the kings of the earth committed sexual immorality, and the ones inhabiting the earth were made drunk from the wine of her sexual immorality. 3. And he carried me off in the spirit into a desert: and I saw a woman sitting upon a scarlet wild animal being full of blasphemous names, having seven heads and ten horns. 4. And the woman having been clothed with purple cloth and scarlet, and having been adorned with gold and precious stone, and pearls, having a golden cup in her hand, full of abominations and uncleanesses of her sexual immoralities. 5. And upon her forehead a name having been written, Mystery, Babylon the Great, the Mother of Prostitutes and Abominations of the Earth. 6. And I saw the woman drinking freely of the blood of the saints, and of the blood of the witnesses of Jesus: and having seen her, I wondered a great wonder. (Revelation 17:1-6)

The Great Prostitute

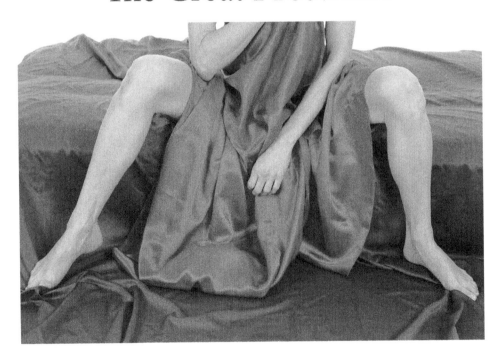

The prophet Zechariah also refers to the great prostitute (Zechariah 5:6-11). The great prostitute is a picture of the religious systems of this world; this includes false Christianity. As such it is one element of the culture of this world that the Bible refers to as Babylon. The great prostitute sitting on the waters indicates the domination of the Babylonian religious system over the world's people. The waters are people, multitudes, nations and tongues (Revelation 17:15).

After the Flood, it wasn't long before men again rebelled against God (Hislop, 1975). A sign that all was not well occurred when Noah lay naked in his tent after becoming drunk on the wine he had made. Ham, his son, saw Noah's nakedness causing Noah to curse Ham's son Canaan (Genesis 9:20-24). It was the Ham side of the family that led the way for others to turn to evil. Cush, one of Ham's sons, was a central figure in the rebellion. Nimrod was the son of Cush (Genesis 10:6, 8). Nimrod's name means 'Rebellion'.

Following the Flood, the animals increased more rapidly than men. A situation arose where wild beasts were terrorising people. Nimrod as a hunter (Genesis 10:8) came to people's rescue. He and the men he led earned the gratitude of people by curbing the inroads of wild beasts attacking. He also gathered many people into a walled city, and this meant that they enjoyed security especially after sunset. However, he became a dominant controlling leader replacing the patriarchal form of leadership, based on families, with a system based on the rule through military might. Many people were willing to accept this in the light of the benefits he had brought.

Nimrod next addressed the fear men had of the God who had flooded the world because of wrongdoing. He set up a system whereby men no longer feared or worshipped the true God. This so-called freedom led to great evil and sexual uncleanness. It was at this point that idolatry and false religion came to mankind.

Nimrod founded a city called Babel. God had said be fruitful and fill the earth (Genesis 9:7). Nimrod and his followers said let us make a name for ourselves, so we are not scattered (Genesis 11:4). They attempted to do this by building Babel. It had a tower upon which were the ancient Zodiac signs. Originally God had written the story of salvation in the stars (Genesis 1:14). The Zodiac, 'Way of Life', was an ancient way of remembering this which was now twisted and perverted with false teaching and a linking of the false to the true. Instead of the Zodiac leading men to the truth, it was used to teach people a lie. One of the reasons why God hates astrology is because it is a perversion of God's purpose in writing His truth in the stars (Bullinger, 1974). The rebellion relied on hidden meanings (mysteries) at first to avoid the opposition of those still faithful to God. As time went on initiation into these mysteries were used to control and deceive people. Part of the initiation system involved drinking an intoxicating cup which made initiates far easier to manage and trick.

Whenever Nimrod went on a hunt, it was in the company of much entertainment. Many young women would accompany him, and much wine drunk with singing. Men were taught to pursue pleasure instead of God. These riotous orgies were very popular amongst many which are the origin of the bacchanalia and the idea that Bacchus was the god of revelry.

At some point, Nimrod came to a sudden and violent end. He was either torn to pieces by wild animals or put to death by those who were still loyal to God. Semiramis was the wife of Nimrod. She was a beautiful but immoral woman. Nimrods death left Semiramis in a vulnerable position regarding leadership. She claimed to conceive a baby without sexual intercourse. She claimed that in a so-called 'virgin' birth she said gave birth to her husband Nimrod reincarnated. Many then began to worship the mother and the child. The ancient mother goddesses' names trace directly back to Semiramis. These ungodly people twisted the promise of God that the seed of women would bruise the serpents head (Genesis 3:15), saying that the seed of the women was the child of Semiramis, Nimrod reborn.

God stepped in confusing the language of men and scattering people around the earth (Genesis 11:7-9). Babel, 'The Gate of God' became known as 'Confusion' and is now called Babylon. As they were scattered, they took the evil system they had created with them. Nimrod was worshipped as Bar-Chus (Son of Cush) or Bacchus who became a chief god amongst the Greeks and Romans. Cush was identified with Hermes the Egyptian synonym for the son of Ham, or Mercury. Nimrod was also known as Ninus. Semiramis was deified as the goddess Rhea or Cybele. She was also known as Aphrodite of Greece and Venus of Rome.

The whole idolatrous religious system came into the world in this way. People were initiated into the mysteries of this religion by drinking from a drugged cup. Jeremiah refers to the drinking of the wine of her fornication (Jeremiah 51:7). The whole earth has been led astray and we still to this day follow much of the Babylonian system of beliefs and practices. The woman in (Zechariah 5:6-11) is pictured hiding in a food basket, so the evil religious system of Babylon polluted the spiritual food of men upon the earth.

The woman being in the wilderness (Revelation 17:4) Isaiah speaks of as the 'desert of the sea' (Isaiah 21:1). Spiritual Babylon is dry and desolate; there is no water of life (Jeremiah 2:13).

Initially, the western empire and its emperor, the beast from the sea, will support the religious system (Revelation 17:3, 4) but ultimately will turn on the system and destroy it (Revelation 17:16). The western empire is a revival of the Roman Empire and not surprisingly this realm of the west is linked to Rome both geographically and religiously.

The Great Prostitute wears purple and scarlet (Revelation 17:4). True purple and scarlet required expensive dyes and clothed only the wealthy, such as queens like Jezebel, or well to do prostitutes, who used purple attire to attract attention. Purple and gold were the apparel of the Roman Emperors and Senators. Also, they are the colours of the garments of the Popes and Cardinals. After the destruction of the city of Babylon the religious system was transferred to Pergamos, hence the Lord saying that Satan's throne was there (Revelation 2:13).

Initiates of the Babylonian religious system migrated from Pergamos to Rome via the Etruscan Plain. Their chief priest lived in Rome with the title Pontifex Maximus. This title was passed on to Julius Caesar when he became Emperor. The title was then passed down to all the Emperors until Constantine who also became head of the Roman Church. In A.D. 378 the Bishop of Rome took the title Pontifex Maximus with the College of Cardinals being equivalent to the pagan College of Pontiffs. Idolatry and false religion also include all that is false even if named Christian. Jesus said that Satan, the enemy sowed tares amongst the wheat and they would only be separated when the end times come (Matthew 13:36-43).

Immorality and idolatry are linked. God accused Israel of an adulterous relationship when they turned from worshipping Him to following idols (Ezekiel 16:15-22). Sexual immorality was often part of the idolatrous acts of worship. It was common for temples to have temple prostitutes (Genesis 38:21).

Paul refers to the post-flood rebellion in (Romans 1). There are four stages of influence the ancient Babel rebellion has upon men. Men had the genuine knowledge of God (Romans 1:21). They turned from God to false religions (Romans 1:23). This rebellion led to gross sexual immorality (Romans 1:26-27). Finally, men's minds became depraved (Romans 1:28-32).

The Beast

7. And the angel said to me, Why have you wondered? I will tell you the mystery of the woman and the wild animal the one bearing her, the one having the seven heads and the ten horns. 8. The wild animal, the one you saw, was and is not and is about to go up out of the Abyss and depart into destruction: and the dwellers upon the earth shall wonder, whose names have not been written upon the book of life from the foundation of the world, seeing the wild animal the one who was, and is not, though is. 9. In this way the mind having wisdom. The seven heads are seven mountains where the woman sits upon them. 10. And there are seven kings: five fell, and one is, the other came not yet: and when he comes it is necessary for him to remain a little while. 11. And the wild animal who was, and is not, even he is the eighth, and he is out of the seven, and into destruction he departs. 12. And the ten horns which you saw are ten kings, who have not yet received a kingdom: but they receive authority as kings one hour with the wild animal. 13. These have one purpose, and the power and authority of themselves to the wild animal they will hand over. 14. These shall make war with the Lamb, and the Lamb will conquer them: because he is Lord of lords and King of kings: and the ones with him are called, and chosen, and faithful. 15. And he says to me, The waters which you saw, where the prostitute sits, are peoples, and crowds, and nations, and tongues. 16. And the ten horns which you saw upon the wild animal, these shall hate the prostitute, and having been made desolate they shall make her naked, and her flesh they will eat, and they will burn her up in fire. 17. For God gave into their hearts to do his purpose, to make one mind and give their kingdom to the wild animal until the word of God be finished. 18. And the woman whom you saw is the great city, having a kingdom over the kings of the earth. (Revelation 17:7-18)

Nebuchadnezzar dreamed of a giant statue made of four different metals. The head was gold, the breast and arms were silver, the belly and thighs were bronze and the legs and were iron with feet partly of iron and mixed with clay. God was showing Nebuchadnezzar that up to Christ's coming there would be four major world kingdoms. These were the Babylonians, the Medes and Persians, the Greeks and the Romans (Daniel 2:31-35). After Israel rejected Jesus, God's prophetic timetable was put on hold, and so the Roman Empire ceased to exist. There remained seven years unfulfilled which will see its fulfilment in the Tribulation. It is, therefore, necessary for the fourth empire's revival for the prophecies fulfilment. The beast was, is not and is to come (Revelation 17:8). The Roman Empire came into being in 753 B.C. being ultimately destroyed in AD 476. The revived Western Empire is yet to come. It will be the feet part of Nebuchadnezzar's image with ten toes that will arise. Thus, we see it pictured as a beast with ten horns (Revelation 17:12). The empire will consist of a confederacy of ten kingdoms.

Seven heads, seven mountains (Revelation 17:9). Rome is spoken of again and again as the seven-hilled city. In John's day, no one would have doubted that the city of seven hills was anywhere other than Rome. The annual Roman festival got its name from the seven hills of Rome, Septimontium. The seven heads also refer to seven types of government. Up to John, there were five forms of government in the Roman Empire. These were: kings, consuls, dictators, decemvir and military tribunals. Current with John was the sixth type of government, imperial, initiated by Julius Caesar. The final form of government is yet to be.

Often in the Bible, a kingdom is spoken of both regarding the domain overall but also as the ruler of the nation. So, in the case of Nebuchadnezzar, he was called the head of gold but also his kingdom (Daniel 2:36-38). The beast after initially supporting the religious world systems destroys the religious system replacing it with the worship of himself through the work of the beast from the land (Revelation 13:11-14). In this instance, we see both the revived Western Empire and its leader.

Revelation 18

1. And after these things I saw another angel coming down, having great authority: and the earth was illuminated from his glory. 2. And he called in strength, with a great voice saying, It fell, it fell, Babylon the great, and it became a dwelling place of demons and a prison of every unclean spirit, and a prison of every unclean bird and having been detested. 3. Because from the wine of the anger of her sexual immorality all the nations have drunk, and the kings of the earth committed sexual immorality with them, and the merchants of the earth from the power of her sensuality were enriched. (Revelation 18:1-3)

The Fall of Babylon

Babylon is more than the religious system. It is the whole world system that will be destroyed by the Lord Jesus Christ when He returns (Revelation 18:20). The influence of the culture of Babel permeates every aspect of our societies. As with any culture, it is something we learn unconsciously and take for granted. Knowledge and practice we are unaware of is something that we seldom challenge.

The issue of rule and control by one leader enforcing decisions through military might is a product of Babylon. The use of money and the financial systems we have is rooted in this culture. The Babylonian religion and its practices permeate much of the way the church organises itself. The constant creating of hierarchies and pecking orders is something that began in Babel. The chasing after pleasure and all that is called hedonism began with Babylon.

When there is a move of the Spirit of God for a time the church and its immediate society throw off some of this ungodly culture. However, people very quickly default back to this in a short time. Churches formed when the Spirit moves tend to function more like a body with every member taking a healthy place. As time passes these churches become more 'organised' with professional leadership and a distinct hierarchy. These churches become less flexible in the Spirit of God's prompting and more willing to follow routines and procedures men have designed.

Babylon is fallen (Revelation 18:2). This fall is not just a judgement that will happen but is something that spiritually already has happened. The best efforts of the kingdoms of men have become occupied by every devil, foul spirit and unclean being. Behind the kingdoms of men is the kingdom of Satan (Ephesians 6:12, 13). Mankind keeps trying to make these Babylonian systems work with the same repeated cycles of failure.

What the world needs is to throw off the patterns of rebellion completely. Israel in Jeroboam's day split into two kingdoms. Jeroboam introduced calf worship to the Northern Kingdom. No matter how many times the ruling family changed, Israel kept worshipping the cows. It was their default position, and it took a significant judgement of God to end this practice. So too with the world and its love of the sins of Babylon. They will only cease with the return of the Lord Jesus Christ.

4. And I heard another voice out of the heaven, saying, Come out of her my people, that you might not take part in her sins, and that you might not receive of her plagues. 5. Because her sins were piled up to the heaven, and God remembered her unrighteousnesses. 6. Give to her as she gave to you and give back double to her according to her works: in the cup which she mixed mix to her double. 7. As much as she glorified herself, and lived in sensuality, give so much torment to her and mourning: because in her heart she says, I sit a queen, and I am not a widow, and mourning I will never see. 8. Because of this in one day will come the plagues on her, death, and mourning, and famine: and she will be burned up in fire because strong is the Lord God the one judging her. 9. And they will weep over her, and they will mourn over her, the kings of the earth, the ones having committed sexual immorality with her and having lived in sensuality when they see the smoke of her burning. 10. From far off having stood because of the fear of her torment, saying, Woe, woe, the great city of Babylon, the strong city, because in one hour came your judgement. 11. And the merchants of the earth weep and mourn over her: because their cargo no one buys anymore. 12. Cargo of gold, and of silver, and of precious stones, and of pearls, and of fine linen, and of purple cloth, and of silk, and all citron wood, and every ivory object and every precious wood object, and of bronze, and of iron, and of marble, 13. And cinnamon, and incenses, and ointment, and frankincense, and wine, and olive oil, and fine flour, and grain, and animals, and sheep: and of horses, and of chariots, and of bodies: and souls of men. 14. And the fruit of the strong desire of your soul departed from you, and all the luxurious and bright departed from you, and they will absolutely not be found any longer. 15. The merchants of these things, the ones having been enriched from her, will stand from afar because of the fear of her torment, weeping and wailing. 16. And saying, Woe, woe, the great city, the one having been clothed with fine linen, and purple, and scarlet, and having been covered in gold, and precious stone, and pearls. 17. Because in one hour so great riches were made desolate. And every helmsman, and all the crowd upon the ships, and sailors, and as many as work the sea stood afar off, 18. and were weeping, seeing the smoke of her burning, saying, What is like the great city? 19. And they threw dust upon their heads and were crying, weeping and mourning, saying, Woe, woe, the great city, in which all the ones having ships in the sea were made rich out of her abundance because in one hour she was made desolate. 20. Rejoice over her, heaven, and the holy apostles and the prophets: because God has judged her for her judgement of you.

(Revelation 18:4-19)

The uncleanness of Babylon will be judged (Revelation 18:3).

The self-glory, empire building and gathering of luxuries of this world at others expense will be judged (Revelation 18:7).

The financial systems of this world and their trading will be judged (Revelation 18:11).

All these things will fall therefore the people of God are commanded to not live in these things but in God, (I John 2:15-17). Christians need to come out of Babylon and not live under this ungodly culture. We do this by learning how precious and how beautiful it is to live by God's principles and ways in our lives. It is much easier to replace something when we have something better. The nature of Babylon is that it clouds the judgement of its followers. The more we focus on God and His Word the clearer we see how flawed the systems of this world are and how much better is God's Kingdom.

The peoples of the world will mourn at the passing of the things they have loved.

21. And one strong angel took up a stone like a great millstone, and he threw it into the sea, saying, In this way with violence will be thrown down Babylon the great city, and it will absolutely not be found again. 22. And the voice of harpists, and of musicians, and of flute players and of trumpeters, would never be heard in you again, and every craftsman of all crafts, would never be found in you again: and the voice of the millstone would never be heard in you again. 23. And the light of a lamp would never shine in you again: and the voice of a bridegroom and of a bride would never be heard in you again: because your merchants were the great men of the earth: because in your sorcery they caused all the nations to wander. 24. And in her, the blood of the prophets and of the saints was found, and of all the ones having been slain upon the earth.
(Revelation 18:20-24)

The righteous however will rejoice at the fall of the systems of this world (Revelation 19:1-6). There are four cries of hallelujah: (Revelation 19:1, 3, 4, 6).

Jezebel is a picture of the great whore (2 Kings 9:10).

The smoke rising forever speaks of an eternal judgement upon this world and its rulers both physically and spiritually which the judgement of Edom's leading city (Isaiah 34:10) also highlights.

With the destruction of the great whore and Babylon, a contrast is now drawn between the great whore and the Bride of the Lamb, the Church of Jesus Christ.

It would appear that literally the city of Babylon will be rebuilt before the return of Jesus. It is clear that people standing off and lamenting are looking at a physical city (Revelation 18:10, 21), not just a culture. Isaiah and Jeremiah predicted the permanent destruction of Babylon. Many have spiritualised Revelation 18 because of this. It would seem the perfect fulfilment of Isaiah and Jeremiah's prophecies has yet to happen. It may be that the city will be rebuilt as the capital of the beast from the sea. It will fall just before the return of Jesus giving time for the world to lament the fall of the city before the judgement of Armageddon.

Revelation 19

1. And after these things I heard a great voice of a great crowd in the heaven, saying, Alleluia: the salvation, and the glory, and the honour, and the power unto the Lord our God. 2. Because true and righteous are his judgements: because he judged the great prostitute, who corrupted the earth in her sexual immorality, and he avenged the blood of his servants out of her hand. 3. And a second time they said, Alleluia: And her smoke goes up into the ages of the ages. 4. And the twenty-four elders and the four living beings fell down and worshipped God the one sitting on the throne, saying, Amen: Alleluia. 5. And a voice came out of the throne, saying, Praise our God, all his servants, and the ones fearing him, both the small and the great. 6. And I heard as it were a sound of a great crowd, and as a voice of many waters, and as a voice of strong thunders, saying, Alleluia: because the Lord God Almighty reigned. (Revelation 19:1-6)

The Four Hallelujahs

Hallelujah means 'praise the Lord.' It is an interjective imperative. In other words, it is a command to praise the Lord. The root meaning of Hallelujah is an intensive form of 'to boast.' It was first used in the Bible concerning Sarah's great beauty (Genesis 12:15) when the princes of Pharaoh commended her to Pharaoh.

This chapter gives four reasons for praising the Lord.

Gods Judgements are True and Righteous (Revelation 19:2)

The truth that God is a God of judgement has increasingly become unacceptable both within our society and within the church. It is hard to find teaching about this aspect of God in the atmosphere of an unbalanced overemphasis on the love of God.

How can God be loving if He will not deal with injustice and evil? God judging is something that is praiseworthy. With the churches current emphasis on praising the Lord should we not be consistent and also honour the God of justice and judgement?

One thing is for sure that God's judgement will never be inappropriate or wrongly directed against anyone (Genesis 18:25). People will get what they deserve.

God Avenges the Blood of His Bond Servants (Revelation 19:2)

Vengeance is an issue we cannot handle because it rightly belongs to God (Hebrews 10:30).

The word for vengeance means, (that which proceeds) out of justice. The word for justice can be translated as vengeance and is done so in (Acts 28:4) and (Jude 1:7).

God cares very much how others treat His people. There will be a price to pay for all the persecution of God's people. How people treat God's servants will be how God treats those people (Matthew 25:41-46).

The Smoke of Babylon's Judgement Rises Forever and Ever (Revelation 19:3)

God is eternal and as such His judgement is eternal. We live as mortals within the timeframe of this world. This season is the time when change is possible, and things can change. Repentance is a beautiful thing because it promises something better. When we come into eternity somethings will be fixed forever and cannot change.

The punishment of God is one of these. Jesus said the worm never dies and the fire is not quenched (Mark 9:44,46,48). The story of the rich man being in torment in Hell is sombre because there is no relief, no mercy and he is still there, and it will continue forever (Luke 16:19-31).

The Almighty Reigns (Revelation 19:4)

The fact that God is almighty and is in control means He can do anything He wants, and this means He can administer perfect justice and judgement no matter how many people question His right to do this.

When we stand before God, we need to stand in the righteousness of Jesus and not in our works. It is only the perfection of Jesus and His work upon the cross that gives us solid ground for salvation. We will not be able to debate anything when we appear before Almighty God (Romans 1:16.17).

The Two Feasts

This chapter contrasts two very different feasts.

The Marriage Supper of the Lamb

7. Let us rejoice and exult and give glory to him: because the marriage of the Lamb came, and his wife has prepared herself. 8. And it was given for her to be clothed with fine linen pure and bright: for the fine linen is the righteousness of the saints. 9. And he says to me, Write, Blessed the ones having been called to the wedding dinner of the Lamb, and he says to me, These words of God are true. 10. And I fell before his feet to worship him. And he says to me, see that you do it not: your fellow servant I am, and of your brothers having the witness of Jesus: worship God: for the witness of Jesus is the spirit of prophecy. (Revelation 19:7-10)

God has declared a feast for His people. He has announced an end to death, sin and suffering, (Isaiah 25:6-10).

The Lord is the bridegroom, and the people of God His bride (Matthew 9:15, John 3:29, Psalm 45) and (2 Corinthians 11:2). It is at this point that the church as the bride celebrates the wedding feast.

The wedding process was in three stages. Firstly, the bridegroom entered into a betrothal with his bride. This engagement was a binding contract involving the parents of the bride and the groom with a bridal price paid. Jesus did this for the church when He died on the cross. Secondly, after some time the groom came to the bride's house to take the bride for himself. The bride would go to the groom's house, usually his father's house. When Jesus comes to the air before the Tribulation, it will be to take the church to His Father's house. Thirdly there is a celebratory feast which lasts some days. After the Tribulation and the return of Jesus, there will be such a feast involving the church, Jesus' bride, some virgins and wedding guests.

It is important to realise that the wedding guests are not the bride any more than the virgins are. These are distinct groups of people. The virgins used to greet the bride and accompany her in a bridal procession. The virgins are the nation of Israel (Revelation 7:4-8). After the Jewish people rejected their Messiah, they were like virgins who fell asleep waiting for the bridegroom, their Messiah. During the Tribulation, they will awake. Some are wise and are prepared to welcome the return of Jesus, but others are foolish. The wise can enter the wedding feast, but the unprepared are barred from this (Matthew 25:1-13). The wedding guests include the wise virgins but also those Gentiles who turn to God in the Tribulation (Revelation 7:9-17). They are marked by how they treat God's servants in the Tribulation. The Gentiles who reject the gospel in The Tribulation are called goats, and those who accept the good news of Jesus are the sheep (Matthew 25:31-46).

White linen was the mandatory apparel for entering the holy of holies (Leviticus 16:4). Linen does not cause sweat (Ezekiel 44:18). Sweating links to the curse of sin (Genesis 3:19). We see the people of God arrayed in righteousness, no longer will they bear their transgressions or its consequences. The bride walks free from any and every aspect of the curse occurring from the fall.

The Feast of the Birds of the Air

11. And I saw the heaven having been opened, and behold, a white horse, and the one sitting upon it, being called Faithful and True, and in righteousness, he judges and wages war. 12. But his eyes as the blade of a flashing sword of fire and upon his head many crowns: having a name having been written which no one knows except himself. 13. And having been clothed with a garment having been dipped in blood: and his name is called, The Word of God. 14. And the armies in the heaven followed him upon white horses, having been clothed with fine linen, white and clean, 15. And out of his mouth goes a sharp sword that with it he may strike the nations: and he shepherds them with a sceptre made of iron: and he tramples the winepress of the rage and of the anger of God Almighty. 16. And he has upon the garment and upon his thigh his name, a name having been written, King of kings and Lord of lords. (Revelation 19:11-16)

Jesus is portrayed here as going to war. He is riding a white horse. Roman princes rode white horses in military triumph. Horses are animals of war (Jeremiah 8:6).

White is also symbolic of righteousness and purity (Isaiah 1:18).

The unknown name signifies that no one has power over the Lord Jesus. Ancient magicians claimed that knowing someone's name gave them coercion rights over that person.

It is when Jesus comes to war that we see the winepress of His wrath trodden (Revelation 14:20). Zechariah gives more details of this (Zechariah 14:2-3). Isaiah also referred to blood-stained garments (Isaiah 63:2-4) which were even foretold from Genesis (Genesis 49:10, 11). God's Word is a sword, and Jesus will smite the nations with the words of His mouth (Hosea 6:5). The sword was the Roman symbol of authority over life and death.

The birds of the air feast in (Isaiah 49:26, Zephaniah 1:7) and (Ezekiel 39:17-21).

17. And I saw one angel having stood in the sun: and he cried with a great voice, saying, to all the birds the ones flying in mid-heaven, Come and gather to the dinner of the great God: 18. That you might eat the flesh of kings, and flesh of commanders of thousands, and flesh of strong men, and flesh of horses, and of the ones sitting upon them, and flesh of all, free and also slaves, and small and great. 19. And I saw the wild animal, and the kings of the earth and their armies having been assembled to make war with the one sitting upon the horse, and with his army. 20. And the wild animal was seized, and with this the false prophet having made the signs before him, by which he caused to wander the ones having received the mark of the wild animal, and the ones worshipping his image. Living the two were thrown into the lake of fire the one burning with sulphur. 21. And the rest were killed with the sword of the one sitting upon the horse, the one having gone out of his mouth: and all the birds fed out of their flesh. (Revelation 19:17-21)

The scene immediately preceding the return of Jesus will see all the nations gathered against Jerusalem for battle. The city will have fallen with horrible atrocities having been committed against its inhabitants. Half of Jerusalem will go into exile. It is at this point that Jesus will return not as a babe born in a manger but as the supreme King of kings riding in battle.

As his feet touch the Mount of Olives, there will be an earthquake unequalled in the history of the world that will affect every part of the planet. Mountains will be levelled, and valleys will be filled. The Mount of Olives will split into two with half moving north and half moving south. The Jewish people will escape through the valley formed. The whole area around Jerusalem will be raised up becoming the highest point on the planet.

The effect on the surrounding armies will be equally as devastating. The various nations will turn on one another, and there will be a great slaughter. The bloodshed will range across the entire length of the land of Israel which will give the birds of the air, unlimited food to feast.

So, will the Lord return and save His people Israel.

The Chronology of the Return of Jesus

The events surrounding the return of Jesus. The order of events would appear to be as below: -

The Second Coming

The term second coming does not occur in the Bible. It is an attempt to distinguish between the time when Jesus came to live upon the earth and make atonement for our sins and the time when He will return to rule upon the earth. Jesus has come to the earth many more times than these two. He walked with Adam and Eve in the cool of the day in the Garden of Eden (Genesis 3:8). There were a number of occasions when Jesus appeared to people in the Old Testament times. An example of this was when Jesus appeared to Joshua as the captain of the host of the Lord (Joshua 5:13-15). This captain was not an angel since Joshua worshipped Him. These Old Testament appearances are often called Theophanies or Christophanies. In the New Testament, Jesus appeared to John on the Isle of Patmos (Revelation 1:9, 10).

Biblically there are a number of terms that more accurately express the return of Jesus to rule upon the earth. Two of these are Apokalupsis and Epiphaneia. Apokalupsis means to reveal, unveil, or remove the cover. The word is used right at the start of the book of Revelation, and it gives the book its name. Another example of its use is in (1 Peter 4:13) which talks about the glory of Jesus being revealed. Epiphaneia means to appear or shine forth. Two scriptures where this is used are (Titus 2:13) when Paul highlights the appearing of our Saviour Jesus Christ and (1 Timothy 6:14) talking about the appearing of our Lord Jesus Christ.

Whatever terms are used the Bible clearly teaches that Jesus will return after He left the earth from the Mount of Olives forty days on from His resurrection (Acts 1:10). This leaving people call the Ascension. At the point, Jesus ascended it was promised that Jesus would return in the same way he went (Acts 1:11). In other words, He will physically return. This return will be seen by people and will not be instantaneous but something that is observed over enough time for everybody to watch. Everybody is going to see this not just a few (Revelation 1:7), (Matthew 24:30). His return will be accompanied by great heavenly signs (Matthew 24:29). Jesus will not return alone but will be accompanied by an army of saints and angels.

This event does not take place in a vacuum. In other words, there are a series of events taking place that Jesus comes into and dramatically impacts. Fitting these events into the correct chronological sequence before they occur is not easy. Consider the prophecies surrounding Judas Iscariot. We can see how they all met together after the events happened. Imagine what the Old Testament saints made of prophecies taking about friends betraying, being priced for silver, and a potter's field. I once had a jigsaw that had been sold placed in the wrong box with a picture that had nothing to do with the jigsaw. Making that jigsaw felt a bit like trying to correctly sequence all the prophetic events and scriptures that have not yet been fulfilled.

The Situation Immediately Before Jesus Comes

The Jewish People

These are in great distress being targeted by Satan for total annihilation. A group of Jewish people will have fled to the South of the land of Israel and have found sanctuary in the desert (Revelation 12:13-17). Others will be still in Jerusalem (Zechariah 14:2). Many will have been taken captive (Zechariah 14:2). Other Jewish people will remain scattered across the earth (Isaiah 11:10-12). Sadly, two-thirds of the nation in the land will perish during the time preceding the return of Jesus to the earth (Zechariah 13:8).

The Nations

The armies of the world will converge on the land of Israel. This gathering will be at the instigation of Satan and the two men who serve him, known as the wild animal from the sea (Revelation 13:1) and the wild animal from the land (Revelation 13:11). This unholy trinity release unclean spirits that gather men and their kings (Revelation 16:13-14). The whole land is filled with these armies. The north part of the land is occupied which is characterised by an area known as Armageddon (Revelation 16:16). The central part is occupied with Jerusalem being surrounded (Zechariah 12:1-3). The southern aspect of the land will also be occupied by troops. We know this because when they are destroyed the area of destruction runs the full two hundred miles of the land (Revelation 14:20).

Key Events

At some point, the Jews will cry out for deliverance to Jesus their Messiah.

For two thousand years, Israel as a nation has rejected Jesus as their Messiah. Individual Jews have turned to Him, but the nation as a whole has not. Jewish people were, in the early days of the Apostles proclaiming the gospel, their chief opponents (Acts 9:23, 12:3, 13:50, 14:2, 14:19, 17:5, 20:3 21:27, 23:12, 24:27). They also incited persecution against the early church (Revelation 2:9, 3:9). This rejection and opposition to Jesus will not be forever. Currently, God is saving many Gentile believers to provoke the Jewish people to jealousy (Romans 10:19, 11:11). The day will come when this will end, and the nation will turn to Christ (Romans 11:28-32).

The Jewish leaders who for so long have led their people astray will urge their people to cry out to Jesus for deliverance (Hosea 6:1-3). This process seems to take place over a two-day period (Hosea 6:2). Joel promised there would be an outpouring of God's spirit upon Israel linked to the deliverance of Jerusalem (Joel 2:28-32). Zechariah tells us that a spirit of grace and supplication will be poured out upon the Jewish people. They will mourn when they see Jesus. However, in that day they will find cleansing and atonement (Zechariah 12:10-13, 13:1).

Jesus Wages War Against Israel's Enemies

The military campaign appears to start in the south and proceed northwards. Jesus is spoken of as travelling from Bozrah and coming from Edom (Isaiah 63:1-6). In coming to Jerusalem, the words that Jesus spoke about the cities inhabitants blessing Him will be fulfilled (Matthew 23:37, 38)

As His feet stand upon the Mount of Olives, it shall split into two with half moving north and half moving south. This valley shall make a way of escape for the hard-pressed residents of Jerusalem (Zechariah 14:3-5).

Jesus shall then move northwards to Armageddon where the beast and the false prophet shall be taken, and his armies totally defeated. These two beasts we are told will be cast alive into the Lake of Fire (Revelation 19:20). It should be noted that where Paul talks about a wicked one being revealed and then consumed with the spirit of Jesus' mouth is not referring to the wicked one being killed (2 Thessalonians 2:8). The word consumed means to use up or destroy. Some versions incorrectly translate this verse slay or kill.

It would appear that Jesus alone wars against these enemies (Isaiah 63:3) and the weapon He uses are His words. He is God. As the earth was made by words from God (Genesis 1:3, 6, 9, 14, 24, 26,) so Jesus destroys His enemies with a word. At the words of Jesus, the blood in His enemies' bodies will be poured out. So great will be the number of troops that the bloodshed will be like squeezing juice from grapes in a wine press. There will be a sea of blood stretching the full two hundred miles of the land of Israel. The blood will be up to a depth of the horses' bridles. Such is the awesome power of Jesus and the terrible anger of God.

More details are given of the process whereby the enemies of Jesus perish in (Zechariah 14:12-15). We are told that while people are standing their flesh shall consume away, their eyes will consume away in their eye sockets and their tongues will consume away in their mouths. Such will be the terror of this that the armies will turn upon one another in murderous warfare.

Seventy-Five Days

After Jesus returns to the earth, there are seventy-five days of essential events introducing the Millennium. We know this because the prophet Daniel tells us (Daniel 12:11-12). The Tribulation is seven years long, split into two parts, with each being one thousand two hundred and sixty days. Daniel prophecies one thousand two hundred and ninety days for the ending of the abomination that makes desolate which is thirty days after the Tribulation. In other words, the statue of the beast is removed thirty days after the end of the Tribulation. Daniel goes on to say that those who come to one thousand three hundred and thirty-five days are blessed highlighting another forty-five days making a total of 30 + 45 = 75.

These seventy-five days are part of major changes that begin the Millennium, the thousand -year reign of Jesus upon the earth.

The Gentile Nations Judged

There will be many mortal people living upon the earth at the end of the Tribulation. These are in three distinct groups. There are those that Jesus describes as His brothers (Matthew 25:40) which refers to godly Jewish believers living through the Tribulation. There were 144,000 sealed. When Saul was persecuting Jewish Christians, Jesus spoke of them in such a way as to show he viewed the persecution as being against Him (Acts 9:4). The Jewish people are Jesus' family according to His incarnation. John spoke of Jesus coming to His own when He lived on earth (John 1:11). Jesus referred to His disciples as His brothers when appearing to Mary Magdalene after His resurrection (John 20:17). There will be a group of people spoken of as goats. These are wicked people who followed the beast and the false prophet who survived the Tribulation (Matthew 25:32, 33). The third group who are righteous Gentile believers are called the Sheep (Matthew 25:34-40).

When Jesus returns, He will set up a throne upon earth and judge the living nations dividing the Gentiles into two groupings according to sheep or goats (Matthew 25:31-46). The criteria will be by how individuals have treated His brothers. During the Tribulation, Satan will target the Jewish nation and especially the godly Jewish remnant. It will be impossible to buy or sell without the mark of the beast (Revelation 13:17). Believers, both Jews and Gentiles, will only survive on the kindness of individuals who receive them and their message. The apostles lived on the hospitality of people who received them into their homes when announcing the coming King and his Kingdom when Jesus live upon the earth (Matthew 10:5-15). Only those who reject the beast and his mark will have the courage and desire to show kindness and help fellow believers. The way people treat others is, therefore, a compelling criterion for distinguishing the sheep from the goats.

The outcome of this judgement is that the mortal righteous saints will go into the Millennium. The wicked will not enjoy the Millennium but will ultimately go via Hell into the Lake of Fire. The Millennium starts with only righteous mortal people living upon the earth. We know this because Isaiah describes people living in the Millennium as continuing to age and die but with a significantly extended lifespan (Isaiah 65:20). These righteous mortal believers will, in turn, have children, grandchildren etc. and it is from these that a growing number of unbelievers mixed with godly descendants will form the basis of a final rebellion on earth (Revelation 20:8).

The Jewish People Judged

Not every Jewish person will turn and accept Jesus as their Messiah when He returns. During these early days of Christ's rule, the scattered Jewish people from across the earth will be assembled to meet with Jesus face to face in a desert place. There a new covenant will be made with Israel after the rebels have been purged from the company (Ezekiel 20:34-38). The basis of this covenant will not be as the original covenant with the Jewish nation. Their first covenant was based on works, but the new covenant is based on God writing His law upon the hearts of the Jewish people (Jeremiah 31:31-34). Israel could not keep the original covenant, but by the grace of God, the new covenant will be maintained.

Revelation 20

1. And I saw an angel coming down out of the heaven, having the key of the abyss, and a great chain upon his hand. 2. And he grasped the dragon, the old snake, who is the Devil and Satan, and he bound him one thousand years, 3. And he threw him into the abyss, and he shut him and sealed over him, that he might not cause the nations to wander still until the thousand years were finished: and after these things, it is necessary for him to be released a little time.
(Revelation 20:1-3)

The Millennium

The Bottomless Pit

The Greek word is abyss or deep. It denotes a place where imprisoned spirits are. The word is used seven times in Revelation (Revelation 9:1, 2, 11; 11:7; 17:8; 20:1, 3). When the legion of demons was cast out by Jesus, they pleaded with Him not to go to the bottomless pit (Luke 8:31). The Abyss, it would appear, is where evil spirits are kept in chains under darkness awaiting their punishment (Jude 1:6).

4. And I saw thrones, and they sat upon them, and judgement was given to them: and I saw the souls of the ones having been beheaded because of the testimony of Jesus, and because of the word of God, and who had not worshipped the wild animal, nor his image, and they received not the mark upon their forehead, and upon their hand: and they lived, and they reigned with Christ one thousand years. 5. But the rest of the dead did not come to life until the thousand years has finished. This is the first resurrection. 6. Blessed and holy the one having a part in the first resurrection: upon these the second has no authority, but they will be priests of God and of Christ, and they will reign with him one thousand years. (Revelation 20:4-6)

Judgement Given to the People of God

The people of God will judge the world and angels (1 Corinthians 6:2, 3).

There are Two Resurrections After the Tribulation

There is a resurrection of the righteous and another resurrection of the wicked. Those righteous saints who died during the Tribulation, after the Rapture of the Church, are resurrected when Jesus returns to reign on the earth. The unrighteous are resurrected one thousand years later after the Millennium (Daniel 12:2, 3) and (John 5:28, 29).

It is clear that the church will be caught up to meet the Lord in the air before the Tribulation and all the church will be resurrected or translated at this point. This happens seven years before these two other resurrections. We see three resurrections in the end times. Three is very much the number associated with resurrection. It was no coincidence that Jesus rose on the third day (1 Corinthians 15:51, 52).

Christ Reigning

This thousand-year reign of Christ on this old fallen earth is known to many as the Millennium. Revelation is often a figurative book, but numbers in the book are very literal. As we saw with the three and a half years equated to 1260 days the book is at pains to give actual numbers even within a pictorial book. This is also seen through the Old Testament prophecies. Also, most figurative scriptures have a literal foundation to them.

The Millennium has been promised in many prophetic scriptures (Revelation 20:2-7, Psalm 2:6-9, Isaiah 65:18-23, Jeremiah 31:12-14, 31-57, Ezekiel 34:25-29, 37:1-13, Ezekiel 40-48, Daniel 2:35, 7:13-14, Joel 2:21-27, Amos 9:13-14, Micah 4:1-7, Zephaniah 3:9-20). Many scriptures can only be fulfilled when Jesus reigns on the earth.

The Millennium begins with Satan being bound in the Abyss for a thousand years (Revelation 20:2-3)

Only righteous saints will enter the Millennium Kingdom (Isaiah 60:21). Isaiah states that it is the righteous who possess the land forever. This righteous company will consist of mortal Jews and Gentiles (Isaiah 65:20).

All the promises of Israel inheriting their land will be fulfilled at this time (Genesis 28:13-14).

A new temple will be built (Ezekiel 40-48). The temple will be with a restored priesthood and sacrifices. The sacrifices look back at Jesus' finished work in a similar way Christians break bread to remember Jesus' death and resurrection. This building will be Israel's final temple, and it will be larger than any previous one.

Jesus will reign upon the throne of David. God promised David that his descendant would reign forever (2 Samuel 7:12-13, 22:51).

Resurrected believers will reign with Jesus at this time (Revelation 3:21).

The earth and its people will be physically blessed. The deserts will bloom (Isaiah 35:1-2), rain and food will be abundant (Isaiah 30:23-24).

Animals will live peacefully with one another and people (Isaiah 11:6-7). Men and women will live a lot longer (Isaiah 65:20), the sick will be healed (Isaiah 33:24) and there will be abundance materially and also emotionally (Jeremiah 31:12-14).

Jesus will rule over all the earth (Isaiah 2:2-4) with a perfect government (Isaiah 9:6-7) bringing peace to the whole (Micah 4:3-4).

The earth will be full of the knowledge of the Lord as the waters cover the sea (Isaiah 11:9).

The Holy Spirit will indwell all believers and be very manifest in the earth (Isaiah 44:3). The glory of God will be seen all over Jerusalem (Isaiah 4:5).

Obedience will be on God's law written in men's hearts, not in an attempt of external works (Jeremiah 31:33).

Israel will be gathered coming down a road to their land called the Way of Holiness (Isaiah 35:8-10).

The world will worship Jesus (Malachi 1:11).

This is the time when the lion will lay down with the lamb (Isaiah 11:1-9).

Water will be abundant in the dry places (Isaiah 35:6-7)

Weapons will become farm implements, and there will be no more war (Isaiah 2:4)

Each year the nations will go up to Jerusalem to keep the Feast of Tabernacles (Zechariah 14:6).

The nations will help the Israelites return to the Land of Israel (Isaiah 60:4).

The wealth of the nations will come to Israel (Isaiah 60:5).

7. And when the thousand years have finished, Satan will be released out of his prison. 8. And he will go out to deceive the nations the ones in the four corners of the earth, Gog and Magog, to bring them together to war: of whom the number is as the sand of the sea. 9. And they went up upon the breadth of the earth, and they surrounded the encampment of the saints and the beloved city: and fire came down from God out of the heaven and devoured them. 10. And the devil, the one deceiving them, was thrown into the lake of fire and sulphur, where the wild animal and the false prophet are: and they will be tortured day and night into the ages of the ages. (Revelation 20:7-10)

Gog and Magog

At the end of the Millennium, there will be one final rebellion of men after Satan comes from the Bottomless Pit. Men have no excuse because mankind will still rebel even in the excellent environment and conditions of the Millennium. This judgement on Gog and Magog is not the same as (Ezekiel 38, 39). When Gog and Magog fell on the mountains of Israel, as recorded by Ezekiel, the sixth part of them remained, but here they are all devoured by fire. Those who fall before the Millennium, the birds ate. When Gog and Magog fell the first time, the promise was that Israel would know the Lord. After the Millennium, they already know their Lord.

The Great White Throne

11. And I saw a great white throne, and the one sitting upon it, from whose face fled the earth and the heaven: and a place was not found for them. 12. And I saw the dead, small and great, having stood before God: and books were opened: and another book, which is the book of life: and the dead were judged out of the things having been written in the books, according to their works. 13. And the sea gave up the dead in it, and death and hell gave up the dead in them: and they were each judged according to their works. 14. And death and hell were thrown into the lake of fire: this is the second death. 15. And if anyone was not found having been written in the book of life he was thrown into the lake of fire. (Revelation 20:11-15)

Christians' names are in the book of life (Philippians 4:3). We, therefore, need not fear this final judgement. We stand before the judgement seat of Christ, not the great white throne. Here we will not be condemned, but our works will be tried for a reward, not judgement (2 Corinthians 5:10).

Those who stand before the great white throne are judged according to their works. These are those who rejected the sacrifice of Jesus upon the cross for it is those of the final resurrection, the resurrection of the wicked, who are judged. His righteousness is not accounted to them. There can be only one outcome for man standing before God without the clothing of Jesus' righteousness, and that is guilty.

It is essential to distinguish between the Bottomless Pit (the Abyss), Hell and the Lake of Fire. The Lake of Fire was initially for the Devil and his angels, and it is a place of eternal punishment (Matthew 25:41). However, men who reject Jesus will also go there. Hell is not forever but is a place where men go after death who have rejected Jesus (Luke 16:22, 23). In many ways, it is like a prison where the inmates have been found guilty but are awaiting sentence. The Bottomless Pit (Abyss) is a place for fallen angels and evil spirits where they wait imprisoned (1 Peter 3:19, 20).

The old creation will then be burned up (2 Peter 3:10).

Revelation 21

1. And I saw a new heaven and a new earth: for the first heaven and the first earth had passed away, and the sea is no longer. 2. And I John saw the holy city, new Jerusalem, coming down from God out of heaven, having been prepared as a bride having been adorned for her husband. 3. And I heard a great voice out of heaven saying, behold, the Tabernacle of God with men, and he will pitch a tent with them, and they will be his people, and God himself will be with them, their God. 4. And God will wipe away every teardrop from their eyes: and death will not be, neither mourning, nor outcry, nor will pain still be because the first things departed. (Revelation 21:1-4)

The Eternal State

There will be a new heaven and earth

The process whereby this happens involves the current heavens and earth being burned up (2 Peter 3:10). Peter talks about us looking and hastening the coming of the day of God. Some people have taken this to mean that we can speed up the arrival of this day by ensuring the Gospel is proclaimed right across the earth. Usually, people further support this view by quoting (Matthew 24:14).

While it is undoubtedly right and desirable to preach the Gospel, is the timing of the coming of the Lord dependant on the works of men? Some Jewish people teach that if there is one day when the whole Jewish nation keep the law entirely that the Messiah will come. All of this seems to emphasise law and works rather than grace. Not only is this very legalistic but it puts men in the driving seat of the timetable of God and replaces the sovereignty of God with the whims and quirks of fallen men.

Looking more closely at the word 'to hasten' (speudo) when using the verb transitively, that is with an object, 'the Day of God' the word means 'earnestly desiring' (Vine, 1973, p. 197). The Revised Version accurately translates the word, 'earnestly desiring.' The often-quoted need to preach the gospel to the whole world and then the end coming refers to the Tribulation saints, not the church. God's sovereign timetable is governed by His will not the works of men.

Since there is going to be a new heaven and earth we see clearly that this world will not last. Many people are trying to save the planet. While it is right to steward what God has given us, it is clear that much has already gone and much more is going. The fact of the matter is that given the conditions at the end of the Tribulation even the Millennium will not replace the need to recreate the heavens and the earth. Christians would do well to put their energies into proclaiming the gospel of Jesus Christ instead of being drawn into a humanistic attempt to save the planet.

Because this world and all that is in it is passing away, how foolish is it to be preoccupied with the things of this world. We need to look for the world that is to come (Hebrews 11:13-16).

There is No More Sea

The sea is used figuratively of the wicked (Isaiah 51:20, 21). So, we see a new earth where the evildoers are no more, a place of peace and rest without trouble (2 Peter 3:13). As the figurative and the literal are both found in the book of Revelation, we see that the new earth will not have seas and oceans in the way the current one has. The implication then is that the new planet will be very different from the current one. Twenty-four-hour light in the city will also give a very different kind of environment (Revelation 21:25). While it is never dark in the city, it is not clear from this passage if day and night continue elsewhere on the earth.

The New Jerusalem

The description of the New Jerusalem is a picture of the glorified people of God from across all ages (Hebrews 12:22) and (Galatians 4:26) which includes Old Testament Saints, the Church and the Tribulation Saints. In eternity any distinctions in the purposes of God for different groupings of His people will be removed.

Jerusalem in Hebrew means double peace. The word is in the dual number so that the name could translate as peace, peace. What double peace will be the people of God's inheritance forever!

The New Jerusalem is a bride prepared for her husband. The church is the bride of Christ (Ephesians 5:25-27). However, in other contexts, the nation of Israel is also described as married to the Lord (Hosea 3:1).

In the eternal state, our dwelling place will be on the new earth for this is where the city comes to rest. From Adam and Eve, God linked people to the earth.

God is going to live with us. There are many benefits of this, but three are specifically highlighted. These are no more tears, no more death, and no more pain.

5. And the one sitting upon the throne said, Behold, I make all things new. And he says to me, Write: because these words are true and faithful. 6. And he said to me; They have happened. I am the Alpha and the Omega, the beginning and the end. I will give to the one thirsting of the spring of the water of life freely. 7. The one conquering will inherit all things, and I will be to him God, and he will be to me a son. 8. But the cowardly, and unbelieving, and the detestable ones, and murderers, and sexually immoral, and sorcerers, and idolaters, and all liars, their part will be in the lake burning with fire and sulphur, which is the second death. (Revelation 21:5-8)

There is a need to overcome to inherit the blessings of God. The word means to conquer or be victorious. We cannot do this in our strength, but by the grace of God, we can be victorious over anything that comes against us. God says we will never be tempted above what we can overcome (1 Corinthians 10:13). We also know that God will crush Satan beneath our feet (Romans 16:20). So, like John, we have confidence that we can overcome the world despite all that we face that causes us pain and discomfort (1 John 2:13, 14, 4:4, 5:4).

There is a list of those who will not inherit the blessing of God. These are the:

Cowardly (Timid, fearful) - An example of this would be those who deny the Lord because of the consequences or persecution (Matthew 10:33)

Unbelieving (Not believing, literally 'not faith') - The only way to please God is through faith in the Lord Jesus Christ (Hebrews 11:6)

Abominable (To stink) - God finds sinful acts abominable. For example, idolatry is something God calls an abomination (Deuteronomy 27:15).

Murderers - This also includes hatred against another. The intent is also something that makes people guilty even if they do not follow it through with the action (Matthew 5:21,22)

Immoral Persons - We get our word pornography from this word. It refers to any form of sex outside of marriage and also includes unclean thoughts as well as actions (1 Corinthians 6:12-20).

Sorcerers - This is referring to those who use drugs to engage with evil spirits. Dabbling with the occult is very wrong, and drugs used in this way can open the door to the demonic. We should shun all of these things (Galatians 5:20).

Idolaters - We are to worship God and not another. We must beware of the many variations of idol worship in the world. It is even possible to view Christian leaders in an idolatrous way. All forms of covetousness are idolatry (1 John 5:21).

Liars - We must speak and follow the truth. The Devil is a liar, and we should not walk in his ways (1 John 1:6-8).

We would do well to shun all of these lest we deceive ourselves that we are genuine believers and followers of Jesus Christ but in reality, are not (2 Corinthians 13:5).

9. And one of the seven angels of the ones having the seven-bowls fill of the last plagues came to me, and he spoke with me. Saying. Come, I will show you the bride, the Lamb's wife. 10. And he carried me off in the spirit upon a great and high mountain, and he showed to me the great city, the holy Jerusalem, coming down out of heaven from God. 11. Having the glory of God: and her light was like a precious jasper stone being clear as crystal. 12. And having a great and high wall, having twelve gates, and upon the gates twelve angels, and the names having been written, which are the twelve tribes of the sons of Israel. 13. From the east three gates: from the north three gates, from the south three gates: and from the west three gates. 14. And the wall of the city having twelve foundations and in them the names of the twelve apostles of the Lamb.
(Revelation 21:9-14)

Having the Glory of God (Revelation 21:12)
How amazing that we will be glorified with the glory of God (Philippians 3:20, 21).

Walled About (Revelation 21:12)
The people of God enjoy the protection of the Lord forever (Job 1:10).

Twelve Gates and Twelve Foundations (Revelation 21:12).
The twelve gates are the twelve tribes of Israel, and the twelve foundations are the twelve apostles. Both the redeemed of Israel and the Gentiles are part of this Bride, (Romans 11:25). Another way of viewing this imagery is that the law was the tutor that brought us to Christ and this was given to Israel, (Galatians 3:24). The Twelve Apostles of the Lamb, are foundational in establishing the church, (1 Corinthians 3:10).

15. And the one speaking with me was having a golden reed, which he might measure the city, and the gates, and her wall. 16. And the city set square, her length as much as also the breadth: and he measures the city with the reed at twelve thousand stadia. The length and the breadth and the height of her are equal. 17. And he measured her wall, one hundred and forty-four cubits, a measure of a man, which is also an angel. 18. And the foundation of her wall was jasper: and the city pure gold, like pure crystal. 19. And the foundations of the wall of the city having been adorned with all precious stone. The first foundation, jasper: the second, sapphire: the third, chalcedony: the fourth, emerald: 20. The fifth, sardonyx: the sixth, sardius: the seventh, chrysolite: the eighth, beryl: the ninth, topaz: the tenth, chrysoprase: the eleventh, hyacinth (aquamarine): the twelfth, amethyst. 21. And the twelve gates, twelve pearls: in turn, each one of the gates was of one pearl: and the street of the city pure gold, as clear glass. 22. And an inner temple I did not see in her: for the Lord God Almighty and the Lamb is her inner temple. 23. And the city has no need of the sun, neither the moon, that they might shine in her: for the glory of God gave her light, and her lamp is the Lamb. 24. And the nations of the ones being saved shall walk about in her light: and the kings of the earth bring their glory and honour into her. 25. And her gates never will be closed by day: for night will not be there. 26. And they will carry the glory and the honour of the nations into her. 27. And they will absolutely not enter into her any defiling and doing something detestable and false: but only the ones having been written in the book of life of the Lamb. (Revelation 21:9-27)

Foursquare (Revelation 21:16)
The sanctuary in Solomon's temple was foursquare, (1 Kings 6:20). The people of God will be in the dwelling place of God and will be His dwelling place, (Revelation 21:3)

Full of Precious Metal and Jewels (Revelation 21:18, 19).
The people of God are precious to the Lord and were costly to redeem, (Psalm 45:13-15)

Gates of Pearls (Revelation 21:21)
The entrance was expensive. It cost the Lord Jesus everything; He had to pay the price for our entrance, (Matthew 13:46). A pearl is slowly formed when a piece of grit finds its way into an oyster. Slowly the gravel is coated by the oyster, and the pearl shaped. It builds through the suffering of the oyster. Entrance into the blessing of God has only been because of the pain of the Lord Jesus, (Hebrews 5:8).

The Measurements of the City

The city is foursquare, in other words, it is cubic. The holiest of holies in the temple was a perfect cube (1 Kings 6:19-20). The people of the city will dwell with God in the holiest of the holy. The city is enormous being 1, 380 miles long, wide and high. Dropped upon the United States, it would cover from Canada to the Gulf of Mexico and spread from the Atlantic Ocean to Colorado. It has been estimated that if 20 billion people reside in the city, each person would have one-thirtieth of a cubic mile each, about a cube of seventy-five acres per person (Morris, 1983, pp. 450-451).

Revelation 22

1. And he showed me a pure river of water of life, bright as crystal, going out of the throne of God and the Lamb. 2. In the middle of her street, also on this side and that side of the river, the tree of life, producing twelve fruits, they give back its fruit according to one each month, and the leaves of the tree for healing the nations. 3. And every curse will not be any longer: and the throne of God and of the Lamb will be in her: and his servants will serve him. 4. And they will see his face: and his name will be upon their foreheads. 5. And night will not be there: and they have no need of a lamp and light of the sun: because the Lord God gives them light: and they will reign into the ages of the ages. (Revelation 22:1-5)

There is a River of Life and a Tree of Life (Revelation 22:1). The tree of Life lost in the fall God here restores (Genesis 3:22-24). Eternal life is given to the church (John 4:10). Hope fulfilled is likened to a tree of life (Proverbs 13:12). Every hope of the people of God will happen (Hebrews 6:18, 19). Christian hope is not a forlorn hope it is an absolute sure thing.

The Conclusion

6. And he said to me, These words are faithful and true: and the Lord God of the holy prophets sent his angel to show his servants what it is necessary to happen quickly. 7. Behold, I come quickly. Blessed the one keeping the words of the prophecy of this book. (Revelation 22:6-7)

These words are faithful and true. Unlike the words of men, the Word of God will happen. His word is so reliable that by His Word the World was formed (Genesis 1:3, 6, 9, 11, 14, 20, 24, 26, 29). God's words are pure like silver refined seven times (Psalm 12:6). So, potent are the words of Jesus when He returns it will be with words that He smites and overthrows His enemies (Revelation 19:15). Given the reliability of God's Word, it is utter folly to question it and to believe the lies of men.

We are told that what God has said will happen soon and Jesus will come quickly. 'Soon' means with quickness and speed. In other words, Jesus' return will be sudden and take people by surprise. It is essential that we are prepared and not caught unawares. The word translated 'quickly' means without delay or before long. Since two thousand years have passed His coming must be very near indeed if it was near when John wrote Revelation. We should, therefore, live with expectancy day by day looking for Jesus' return.

The only way to be truly prepared for the coming of Jesus is to keep His words. The only way we can keep His words is to believe in Him (John 6:29). If we say we believe in Him but it does not affect the way we live our lives than we are deceiving ourselves (James 2:20-26).

8. And I john the one seeing these things and hearing. And when I heard and saw, I fell to worship before the feet of the angel of the one showing to me these things. 9. And he says to me. See that you do it not: for I am your fellow servant, and of your brothers the prophets, and of the ones keeping the words of this book. Worship God. 10. And he says to me, Do not seal the words of the prophecy of this book: because the time is near. 11. The one harming let him harm still: and the one being filthy let him be filthy still: and the righteous one let him be righteous still: and the holy one let him be holy still. (Revelation 22:8-11)

There is only one person who it is right to worship, and that is God. In other words, we should worship the Father, the Son and the Holy Spirit (Exodus 20:4-6). We are very prone to fall down and worship others and other things. In our celebrity culture, many are worshipping others. Alas, this attitude has also invaded the church. Many follow after famous speakers and often much talk is about famous leaders. We need once again to focus on the Lord Jesus and His Word, not on men or their organisations. There is far too much promoting of our churches and their programs at the expense of the Gospel. We should put Jesus at the centre of all we do and say.

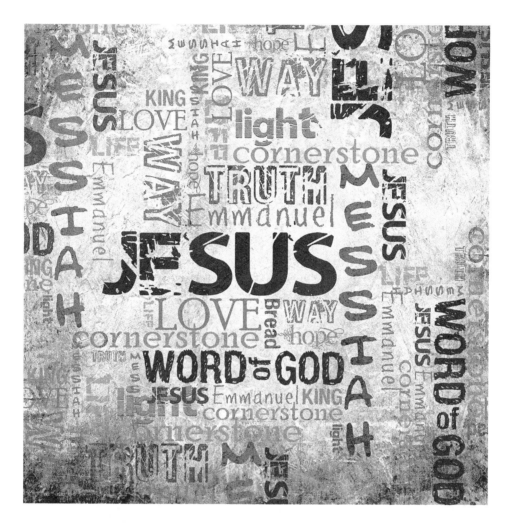

The words of this prophecy are unsealed (Revelation 22:10). When Daniel prophesied his words were sealed because the time for their fulfilment was distant. People could not understand these words because the time for understanding hadn't come (Daniel 12:4). However, when Jesus came, the time to understand Daniel's words had also come and Jesus unsealed these words (Matthew 24:15). It is very clear that God wants us to understand the words of Revelation because they have been left unsealed. There has been a concerted effort by Satan to convince Christians that they cannot understand this book. Yet God here is at pains to underline the fact that the book is unsealed.

12. And behold, I come quickly: and my reward with me, to give to each as his work will be. 13. I am the Alpha and Omega, beginning and end, the first and the last. 14. Blessed the ones doing his commandments, that their right will be to the tree of life, and they may enter through the gates into the city. 15. But outside the dogs, and the sorcerers, and the sexually immoral, and the murderers, and the idolaters, and everyone loving and doing a lie. 16. I Jesus sent my angel to witness to you these things for the assemblies. I am the root and offspring of David, the bright and morning star. (Revelation 22:12-16)

There is a reward to be won by the way we respond to what is said in the book of Revelation and to the Lord Jesus Christ. We should live constantly aiming to win this reward. Of recent years the Church has focused much more on the here and now. There have been some benefits in doing this. The downside of overemphasising this is that people lose sight of the prize that they need to gain. Since the here and now is only for a little while but God's reward is forever it is reasonable to give a lot of attention to what lies ahead. Indeed, a great motive for the way we live now is to win the future reward (1 Corinthians 9: 24-27).

17. And the Spirit and the bride say, Come. And the one hearing, let him say, Come. And the one thirsting let him come. And the one wanting let him receive the water of life freely. 18. I demonstrate to be true for each one hearing the words of the prophecy of this book, if anyone adds to these, God will add upon him the plagues the ones having been written in this book. 19. And if anyone takes away from the words of the prophecy of this book, God will take away his part from the book of life, and out of the holy city, and of the things having been written in this book. 20. The one testifying these things says, Yes, I come quickly. Amen. Yes, come quickly Lord Jesus. 21. The grace of our Lord Jesus Christ be with all of you. Amen. (Revelation 22:17-21)

There are two things to be avoided in our response to what God says to us in Revelation. We should not add to what He has said, and we should not take away from what He has said. Eve, when tempted by Satan, added to the Word of God in her response to Satan, (Genesis 3:3). God had said that Adam and Eve should not eat of the tree, but Eve added that they should not touch it. Adding to what God says leads to legalism. The problem with legalism is that sooner or later we throw off the rules and regulations. In Eve's case when she threw off the man-made law of not touching the tree she also threw aside the God-given instruction not to eat the fruit.

Taking away from what God says leads to the opposite problem of legalism which is license. An example of this was when the Israelites made a golden calf despite God having just told them not to make images to worship which resulted in the people running out of control, (Exodus 32:25).

The way we respond to the invitation to come is to take God at His word without either legalism or license. Let us be people who are thirsty for God and His righteousness and let us come to Him and simply take Him at His word. As such we shall enjoy His eternal reward with Him forever.

Bibliography

Anderson, S. R., 1975. The Coming Prince. Grand Rapids Michigan: Kregel Publications.

Bullinger, E., 1974. The Companion Bible. London: Samuel Bagster.

Bullinger, E. W., 1974. The Witness of the Stars. Grand Rapids, Michigan: Kregel Publishing.

Bullinger, E. W., 1975. Number in Scripture. Grand Rapids, Michigan: Kregel Publications.

Edersheim, A., 2014. The Life and Times of Jesus the Messiah. United States: Hendrickson Publishers.

Grant, F. W., 1955. Prophetic History of the Church. New York: Loizeaux Brithers.

Harding, J., 2015. Babylon and the Bretheren. Eugene, Oregon: WIPF & STOCK Publishers.

Hislop, A., 1975. The Two Babylons. London: S. W. Partridge & Co.

Ironside, H. A., 1919. Lectures on the Book of Revelation. Neptune, New Jersey: Loizeaux Brothers.

Lang, G. H., 1945. The Revelation of Jesus Christ: Selected Studies. London: Oliphants.

Lang, G. H., 1973. The Histories and Prophecies of Daniel. Grand Rapids, Michigan: Kregel Publishing.

MacArthur, J., 1989. The MacArthur New Testament Commentary: Matthew 24-28. Chicago: Moody Publishers.

Morris, H. M., 1983. The Revelation Record. Carol Stream, Illinois: Tyndale House Publishers Inc..

Pember, G. H., 1887. The Great Prophecies Concerning the Gentiles, the Jews and the Church of God. London: Hodder and Stoughton.

Pember, G. H., 1976. Earths Earliest Ages. Grand Rapids, Michigan: Kregel Publishing.

Rhodes, R., 2012. The End Times in Chronological Order. Eugene, Oregon: Harvest House Publishers.

Rhodes, R., 2013. 40 Days Through Revelation. Eugene, Oregon: Harvest House Publishers.

Rhodes, R., 2017. Bible Prophecy Answer Book. Eugene, Oregon: Harvest House Publishers.

Rhodes, R., 2018. Israel on High Alert. Eugene Oregon: Harvest House Publishers.

Seiss, J. A., 1900. The Apocalypse: Lectures on the Book of Revelation. New York: Cosimo Classics.

Tatford, F. A., 1947. Prohecy's Last Word. London: Pickering and Inglis Ltd..

Tatford, F. A., 1971. The Prophet of the Mystle Grove. London: Prophetic Witness Movement International.

Thomas, D. R. L., 1992. Revelation 1-7: An Exegetical Commentary. Chicago: Moody Press.

Vine, W. E., 1973. An Expository Dictionary of New Testament Words. London: Oliphants.

Walvoord, J. F., 1979. The Rapture Question. Grand Rapids, Michigan : Zondervan Publishing House.

Made in the USA
Coppell, TX
23 July 2020